LADY BIRD JOHNSON

MODERN FIRST LADIES

Lewis L. Gould, Editor

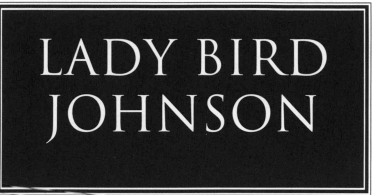

LADY BIRD JOHNSON

OUR ENVIRONMENTAL FIRST LADY

LEWIS L. GOULD

UNIVERSITY PRESS OF KANSAS

© 1988, 1999 by the University Press of Kansas

All rights reserved

Published by the University Press of Kansas
(Lawrence, Kansas 66049), which was organized by
the Kansas Board of Regents and is operated and
funded by Emporia State University, Fort Hays State
University, Kansas State University, Pittsburg State
University, the University of Kansas, and Wichita
State University

Library of Congress Cataloging-in-Publication Data

Lady Bird Johnson : our environmental First Lady /
edited by Lewis L. Gould.

p.   cm. — (Modern first ladies)

Includes bibliographical references and index.

ISBN 0-7006-0992-x (cloth : alk. paper)

1. Johnson, Lady Bird, 1912–   .   2. Presidents'
spouses — United States Biography.

3. Environmental protection — United States.

4. Roadside improvement — United States.

I. Gould, Lewis L.   II. Series.

E848.J64L33   1999

973.923′092 — dc21

[B]   99-32508

British Library Cataloguing in Publication Data
is available.

Printed in the United States of America

10 9 8 7 6 5 4 3 2 1

The paper used in this publication meets the
minimum requirements of the American National
Standard for Permanence of Paper for Printed
Library Materials z39.48-1984.

CONTENTS

EDITOR'S FOREWORD

The Modern First Ladies series seeks to fill a major gap in the study of presidential wives in the twentieth century. Although there have been individual biographies of several of the prominent First Ladies who have held that position since 1900, there is a noticeable absence of books that consider the role of these women in the White House in a systematic and analytical way. This series endeavors to provide general readers and scholars with reliable, well-researched, thoughtful treatments of what the First Ladies did during their time in Washington, what their historical impact was, and how they contributed to the evolution of an institution that occupies a unique place in the government of the United States.

The individual volumes in the series will look closely at the performance of the First Lady in the varied roles—ceremonial, personal, political, and substantive—that she is asked to play. The primary focus will be on the years when her husband was president and when she discharged the duties and experienced the burdens that every First Lady confronts. The authors will consider how these women interacted with the public, the issues and causes, if any, with which they were identified, and the controversies and problems that they faced in the White House. Each book will relate the individual First Lady to the history of women in the United States and to the evolution of the presidency in the twentieth century. The volumes will provide for the first time a sound basis upon which to make meaningful comparisons among the First Ladies and to gauge with more precision their impact on American history. The result will be a better understanding of how First Ladies have achieved their special place in the government, politics, and cultural life of the United States.

PREFACE

This book is an outgrowth of an earlier study on *Lady Bird Johnson and the Environment*, published by the University Press of Kansas in 1988. In the decade since the book first appeared, the study of First Ladies has claimed greater attention among scholars of women's history and the history of the American presidency. Once I decided as the general editor to embark upon the series of volumes on the Modern First Ladies, of which this book will be the first, it seemed appropriate to return to the study of Mrs. Johnson and to revise it to fit the format of the new series.

Lady Bird Johnson and the Environment explored several issues, most notably the battle over the enactment and enforcement of the Highway Beautification Act of 1965, in detail. In the process, the focus on Mrs. Johnson sometimes became obscured in the legislative maneuvering that grew out of this controversial piece of environmental legislation. So busy was she with other aspects of beautifying Washington, DC and in advocating environmental causes that the narrative in other parts of the book also shifted her to the background.

This shorter, more concentrated treatment endeavors to put Lady Bird Johnson at the center of events throughout the narrative. It also emphasizes her contribution as one of the most significant First Ladies of this century in shaping the institutional and policy-making aspects of the president's wife. To a greater degree even than Eleanor Roosevelt, Lady Bird Johnson devised and developed the staff, procedures, and tactics that subsequent First Ladies have employed when they have entered the public arena. The institution of the First Lady in its contemporary form stands very much in the aura of the achievements of Mrs. Johnson, Liz Carpenter, Sharon Francis, Bess Abell, and Cynthia Wilson from their White House years between 1965 and 1969.

The ensuing narrative draws freely on the information and the prose in the earlier book, but my approach is different in perspective and attitude. Rather than seeking to establish the legitimacy of studying a First Lady in depth, I try to provide a clear and crisp overview of the actions that made Lady Bird Johnson such an important innovator in the 1960s. The concentration is more on what she did than on the mechanics of how she accomplished her goals. Readers seeking a detailed recounting of the legislative history of her role in highway beautification, for example, should refer to the earlier book. This account seeks to show that her efforts to advance the cause of highway beauty represented a new departure for a First Lady. The same is true for the work she did in beautifying Washington in its monumental areas and in its inner-city ghettos.

Although there has not been a great deal of writing about Mrs. Johnson in a scholarly vein since 1988, some new material has appeared. The ever-expanding field of Lyndon Johnson biography has also grown during the past decade. The release of the Johnson White House audio tapes has been a notable feature, contributing to a better understanding of how the president worked and his relationship with his wife as a political partner. I have made use of that new information when it illuminates the basic story of Mrs. Johnson's role as First Lady.

*　　*　　*

Space does not permit complete thanks to everyone who contributed to the first volume and to this new treatment of Lady Bird Johnson. I owe special thanks first to Mrs. Johnson herself, who allowed me to go through the records of her work in the public materials at the Lyndon Baines Johnson Library with complete freedom. No one at the library ever suggested what interpretation I should adopt or how I should write. Liz Carpenter was always helpful and encouraging. She remains one of the most energetic and witty figures in the history of modern First Ladies. The individuals who worked with Mrs. Johnson were very generous with their time—Bess Abell, Sharon Francis, Stewart Udall, Walter Washington, and Cynthia Wilson.

I could not have completed the original research on this book without the assistance of the staff of the Lyndon Baines Johnson Library. I owe thanks to Harry Middleton, the library's director, and his talented colleagues who assisted my research in so many positive ways during those years. Since 1988 students in my seminars, First Ladies, and Lyndon Johnson and His Times, have provided me with important insights and helpful information. I am grateful to my former graduate students, Christie Bourgeois, Thomas Clarkin, Stacy Cordery, Debbie Cottrell, Patrick Cox, Scott Harris, Byron Hulsey, Jonathan Lee, Mark Young, and Nancy Beck Young for their kindness and support over the past ten years.

The opportunity to work with David Thaxton and his colleagues at Thaxton-Green Studios on a film about Mrs. Johnson was an important stimulus to developing the series of books about First Ladies and to revisiting the book on Mrs. Johnson as a possible volume in the new project. The idea for the series in the first place was the inspiration of my wife, Karen Gould, who has maintained her interest in my work on presidential wives during a decade when illness and family concerns were important claims on her time and energy. She has helped me when my own infirmities made completing this book more of a challenge than I had anticipated.

CHAPTER 1

FROM KARNACK TO THE WHITE HOUSE

"My interest in beauty dates way, way back to my girlhood," Lady Bird Johnson said in 1965. "Some of the most memorable hours I've ever spent have been in the out-of-doors, communing with nature and reveling in the scenic beauty which abounds." She was born Claudia Alta Taylor on 22 December 1912 in Karnack, Texas, a small town of 600 people in Harrison County, near the Louisiana border. It was, she remembered, "just like the Old South transplanted. It was cotton culture — plain, simple, hard country, just like Alabama, Louisiana, and Mississippi." She was the only daughter and third child of Thomas Jefferson Taylor and Minnie Patillo Taylor. Her parents had been married for a dozen years; they had two sons, Tom Jr. and Antonio, who were eleven and eight when Claudia was born.[1]

The baby girl acquired her lifelong nickname in infancy. A black cook said she was "as purty as a lady bird," referring to the ladybird beetles of the region. "It was very early in life and people began to call her Lady Bird," Tony Taylor later recalled; "the poor gal tried to shake it but in vain."[2]

Claudia's parents had two quite different personalities. T. J. Taylor ran a flourishing cotton business and general store, where he proclaimed himself a "Dealer in Everything." He lent out money at 10 percent and when his customers could not pay foreclosed on their land. He built up holdings of thousands of acres between 1900 and 1920. Claudia grew up in the comfortable lifestyle of the Brick House, a distinctive two-story house in Karnack. She remembered that "it was built by slave labor back before the Civil War."[3] Her father dominated the tiny community. The neighbors called him "Mr. Boss" or "Cap Taylor." Friends recalled that he was "a ladies' man" who did not always honor his marriage vows or those of others. His example of assertive masculinity shaped Claudia's own choice of a husband when she met Lyndon Johnson. "He's the only man I've ever met who is taller than my daddy," she said at the time.[4]

Minnie Taylor had only about six years with her daughter and the messages she transmitted were less enduring than those of Claudia's father. An aura of culture, eccentricity, and distance from the ways of Karnack surrounded Mrs. Taylor. "Miss Minnie," said a childhood friend of Claudia's, "wore large Panama hats with a veil tied down under her chin and her dresses were of that Gibson Girl type." She had her own car and chauffeur, and she possessed a large library of the books that middle-class Americans regarded as classics during the early years of the century. Her health was often precarious, and she avoided eating meat. The veils and turbans she wore provided her with relief from chronic migraine headaches and gave her a distinctive appearance in little Karnack.[5]

The rural community in East Texas offered too cloistered a life for Minnie Taylor, and she escaped it whenever she could for cosmopolitan attractions. During the opera season she went to Chicago, and she pursued health remedies and other cures at sanitariums in Battle Creek, Michigan, and elsewhere. Her two sons went to boarding school, and the family was not often together in Karnack. Minnie's resistance to East Texas life may also have expressed itself in invitations to local African Americans to visit her home. She sought out black culture in precincts where other whites never ventured. Residents also remembered that Minnie organized a drive to protect local quail against excessive hunting. During the last summer of her life, she dabbled in politics. Women by then could vote in the Democratic primary, and Mrs. Taylor campaigned against a candidate who had received a draft deferment. He was, she told other women, "a slacker," and he lost.[6]

Claudia's memories of her mother were fleeting: she was "tall, graceful, wore white quite a lot, and went around the house in a great rush and loved to read," an influence that fostered Claudia's lifelong love of books. "She used to read me Greek, Roman, and Teutonic myths. Siegfried was the first romantic hero I ever loved." But their time together was brief. Minnie's health worsened after Claudia was born, the boys went back to private schools, and their mother's nervous breakdown took her again to a sanitarium in Battle Creek. After returning home, at the age of forty-four Minnie Taylor became pregnant. In late summer 1918, the family dog tripped her on the stairs; the fall caused a miscarriage, blood poisoning, and her death in September. Claudia was at first "quite sure" that her mother was going to come back, but in time, with that resilience of children, "I quit even thinking about it at all."[7]

T. J. Taylor did not do well as a single parent, and he accepted the advice of relatives that Effie Patillo, his wife's unmarried sister from Alabama, should take care of Claudia. Aunt Effie, "a lovely little spinster lady," came to Karnack and stayed on as a surrogate mother. "She was delicate and airy and very gentle," her niece later said, and "she gave me many fine values which I wouldn't trade for the world." These gifts included a love of nature and a devotion to reading, akin to that of Claudia's mother. Effie was less successful on the practical side of life. Claudia grew up having to depend on herself in school and on the friends of her own age she made in Texas and Alabama.[8]

She spent much of her time alone and out doors. "I grew up listening to the wind in the pine trees of the East Texas woods," she said in 1976. On Caddo Lake, which was very near the Brick House and Karnack, she "loved to paddle in those dark bayous, where time itself seemed ringed round by silence and ancient cypress trees, rich in festoons of Spanish moss. It was a place for dreams." On her walks she watched the wildflowers and "the daffodils in the yard. When the first one bloomed, I'd have a little ceremony, and name it the queen." She spent summers with relatives in Alabama, "sitting on the porch while the women shelled peas and talked about genealogy, who-married-who and how many children they had."[9]

Claudia went to a one-room schoolhouse in Karnack, and she also spent time in Alabama through her seventh-grade year. She then attended school in nearby Jefferson, Texas, for two years. About this time she spelled "my middle name Byrd, after I had given up

Claudia Taylor as an active teenager. (LBJ Library photograph, B6328)

ever managing to be called Claudia." She went to Marshall, the county seat, where she graduated at fifteen from the local high school. Her good grades made her the likely choice to be valedictorian or salutatorian. But she feared having to make a speech to the commencement audience and made sure that she came in third in the class by a single point.

Her father and Effie Patillo decided that she was too young for college, so instead Claudia went to St. Mary's School for Girls in Dallas. In her two years there, she played Sir Toby Belch in *Twelfth Night* and saw such plays as *They Knew What They Wanted.* Years later she recalled, when talking with composer Richard Rodgers about his show *Carousel,* that it "came from *Liliom* and was one of the very first plays I had ever seen when I was fifteen" and was "part of a seed that yielded my long harvest of joy in the theater." Gradually, her shyness eased a little. In 1930, when she was eighteen, she prepared to go to the University of Texas. Having flown when she lived in Marshall, she readily agreed to take a plane to Austin to inspect her college choice.[10]

"I fell in love with Austin the first moment that I laid eyes on it and that love has never slackened," she later remembered. The natural beauty of the Texas capital enthralled her. "There were bluebonnets with red poppies and primroses among them," she wrote in 1966: "I remember them like a friend." Despite the depression, her father provided Claudia with her own car, an old Buick, and a charge account at Neiman-Marcus. However, he refused to let her join Alpha Phi sorority, which she pledged in her first year.[11]

During four active years, Claudia Taylor chose widely from the curriculum. She took a chemistry course and received the only grade of D on her record. Most of her time was spent in the History Department, but she took a course in geology "which stretched my perspective of the life of man on this physical planet." Already looking ahead to a profession, she added journalism to her program. An article she wrote on the poems of John Keats appeared in the *Daily Texan* in 1933, and she worked as the publicity manager for the University of Texas Sports Association, which ran the women's athletics program. She joined her fellow members for the yearbook picture in the *Cactus.* At the university, she believed, "all of the doors of the world suddenly were swung open to me."[12]

She pursued an active social life and "always had a lot of young men, you know, beaus in those days," as one of her friends put it. Claudia Taylor agreed. Late in her life she observed, "From the time I was seventeen until I left the university, I had all the beaus I could handle. I had a lot of fun. Crazy, wild, city fun. I think I fell in love every April." The men she saw found, as one of them said, "that we had been doing what she wanted to do." Claudia Taylor made it clear that "she was really never serious about anybody who she thought wouldn't amount to something, wouldn't work hard and get there." She decided to stay in Austin after she received her Bachelor of Arts degree, with honors, in June 1933, and to work for a degree in journalism. She also studied shorthand. By June 1934 she had her journalism degree in hand, again with honors. Her plan for the summer was to spend time in Karnack, supervise the redecoration of the Brick House, and see her father. Her long-range plan was to become a drama critic on a newspaper, a formidable ambition during the depths of the depression. By August 1934 she was back in Austin for a stay with her friend Eugenia "Gene" Boehringer, who wanted her to meet a young man named Lyndon Johnson.[13]

On 31 August 1934, Claudia Taylor met Lyndon Baines Johnson. They arranged to have breakfast the next morning. She recalled years later that he was "excessively thin but very, very good looking, with lots of black hair, and the most outspoken, straightforward, determined manner I had ever encountered. I knew I had met something remarkable, but I didn't quite know what." She was a slender woman, about five-feet-four, with dark hair; she had a simple taste in attractive clothes. She had made peace with her nickname by that time; her stationery was personalized with "Bird Taylor."[14]

The young couple spent the day together driving around Austin, and then the twenty-six-year-old Lyndon proposed. "I thought it was some kind of a joke," she said later, but she was intrigued. Johnson gave her a book to mark the occasion. Inside the cover of *Naziism: An Assault on Civilization,* he had written, "To Bird— In the hope within these pages she may realize some entertainment and find reiterated here some of the principles in which she believes and has been taught to revere and respect." A serious study of the Germany of Adolf Hitler, the book was tangible evidence that Bird Taylor and Lyndon Johnson had talked about matters of substance and of the heart at their first meeting.[15]

During the next week, Johnson took Lady Bird to meet his parents and to the King Ranch in South Texas to see his boss, Cong. Richard Kleberg. On his way back to Washington, Lyndon stopped off to see Claudia's father. Measuring Johnson against the men who had visited his daughter earlier, T. J. Taylor said, "You've been bringing home a lot of boys. This one looks like a man."[16]

An intense long-distance romance followed by mail and by telephone. "This morning I'm ambitious, proud, energetic and very madly in love with you," Johnson wrote to her on 24 October 1934. In letter after letter he pressed her to agree to marriage. Her letters told him about the books she was reading and the flowers she had spotted as she walked around Karnack. She told Johnson at one point, "I would hate for you to go into politics" but added at once, "Don't let me get things any more muddled for you than they are though, dearest!" Three decades later, reading through the old letters, she recalled those autumn days when she had been "doing over the Brick House, with all of my days and half of my mind, and with the other half trying to decide whether to marry Lyndon, while we wrote and he telephoned and we headed toward marriage."[17]

The ardent Lyndon Johnson pressured Claudia Taylor to marry him when he drove to East Texas in early November. Aunt Effie urged her to wait, but T. J. Taylor told the couple that her aunt had "no right" to ask his daughter "to sacrifice her life and happiness to wait on her." His advice to them was "you and Bird do as you think best."[18]

The couple decided to drive the several hundred miles to Austin to see Gene Boehringer. On the way, Johnson persuaded Claudia to marry him. He called friends in San Antonio, arranged for a license, and they were married there on the evening of 17 November 1934. "Lyndon and I committed matrimony last night," the new Mrs. Johnson told Boehringer the next morning, before the couple left on a Mexican honeymoon.[19]

What led these two people into marriage? Some of Lyndon Johnson's biographers believe that he pursued Claudia Taylor with such energy and passion because he wanted a wealthy wife. He was probably aware that her family had some money, in contrast to the more precarious circumstances of his own father and mother at that time. Yet a purely mercenary Lyndon Johnson would not have fooled the sharp and intelligent Bird Taylor. She was not a wallflower, someone without a romantic past of her own. Instead, as in most courtships and marriages, an element of mutual advantage was at work beyond the physical and emotional tug between the two young people involved.

Both parties gained from the union. The ambitious Lyndon Johnson had found "the one possible wife" for him and "the ideal helpmate for a going-places politician." For Bird Taylor, Lyndon Johnson, a congressional aide with a bright political future, was also a way out of Karnack and the invisible restraints that limited bright Texas women during the early 1930s. The bridegroom was clearly going somewhere and seemed likely "to get there." The woman who married him made as shrewd a judgment about his long-range prospects as he made about her family's finances.[20]

During the early years of marriage, Mrs. Johnson adjusted to the habits and demands of a hard-driving, self-centered husband. He criticized her taste in clothes, often in front of their friends or even strangers, and he used to say to her, "You don't sell for what you're worth." She had to bring him breakfast in bed, and he did little of the traveling, sightseeing, or reading that they had discussed while courting. At times, his abrasive tongue and his manner toward her embarrassed onlookers. Because the marriage endured for almost four decades, however, excessive emphasis on the inevitable strains in the relationship overlooks a reality of affection and respect to which both Johnsons contributed.[21]

Yet Lyndon Johnson has the reputation, which he personally cultivated, of a man who was, at intervals during his marriage, unfaithful to his wife. He is supposed to have had an affair with Alice Glass Marsh between 1938 and 1941; one other involvement is construed as having shaped his presidential plans in 1960. Johnson also liked to boast of his sexual prowess. When the subject of John F. Kennedy's sexual affairs arose, Johnson asserted: "Why, I had more women by accident than he ever had by design." Some of this talk was typical masculine braggadocio and, in view of Johnson's chronic problems with the truth, should be discounted.[22]

Yet there is evidence that Johnson preyed on some of the women who worked with him, was not above making advances to the wives of friends and reporters, and acted as a kind of romantic predator when his wife was not present. Lady Bird Johnson seems to have taken the position that her husband's dalliances were inherently temporary and unimportant. Since her own father was a well-known philanderer in Marshall, perhaps she applied long-standing personal defensive mechanisms that already existed to her own difficult marital situation. Because a divorce would have meant social disgrace for her and the end of Lyndon's career, patience and calm were the best answers to any rival. "In her realm," Nancy Dickerson observed, "she had no peer; she knew it; he knew it, and so did everybody else."[23]

How long it took and how painful a process it was to reach this degree of acceptance and self-assurance no one but Lady Bird Johnson will ever know. Across three generations, the women in her family grappled with the problem of wayward husbands. That Lady Bird Johnson dealt with it in a way that preserved her marriage and her own emotional stability should not, however, excuse or mitigate the pain, emotional loss, and psychological trauma that Lyndon Johnson imposed by his selfishness and amoral behavior.

After their honeymoon in Mexico, the Johnsons lived in a Washington apartment throughout the first half of 1935. Then in the summer, the Roosevelt administration offered Lyndon the position of Texas administrator for the National Youth Administration (NYA). His wife was in Karnack when he called her to ask, "How would you like to live in Austin?" It was as if he had said, she recalled, "How would you like to go to heaven?" They spent the next two years in Austin for the NYA, a job at which Lyndon was a resounding success. "Not many things have ever meant so much to us as the NYA," she believed, "brief though it was."[24]

In February 1937 the congressman from the Tenth District, James P. Buchanan, died of a sudden heart attack, and Lyndon Johnson wanted to run in the special election to be held in early April. Among the central problems was the immediate need for enough money to launch the campaign until fund-raising from other sources could begin. After talking with former state senator Alvin J. Wirtz, one of her husband's mentors, Lady Bird Johnson was convinced that Lyndon had a chance to win in the crowded field. She called her father and obtained $10,000 from her mother's estate over the weekend. In the campaign itself, she played the supporting role that custom demanded of political wives and "kept the home fires burning." On election day, Lyndon was in the hospital with appendicitis, and she occupied her time, as he suggested, "by taking friends and kinfolks and homebound elderly citizens to the polls and telephoning." Johnson defeated his opponents, "and that ushered in a new chapter in our lives." [25]

Over the next four years, Lyndon poured his energies into work for the Tenth District and into pursuit of his ambition for higher political office. According to his wife, "The biggest word in my vocabulary, the most important was 'constituency,' which one spelled in capitals." She escorted visitors from the Tenth District to the tourist attractions of Washington, "and I spent my hours going to innumerable weddings, gatherings, and in the first year or so paying calls." She also began a lifelong education in the intricacies of Texas politics. Friends recalled Lady Bird Johnson as "a sweet-looking, dark-haired, dark-eyed girl who seemed to adore her husband and let him have the floor." The Johnsons meanwhile wanted to have children, but Mrs. Johnson suffered several miscarriages in the prewar period.[26]

When Johnson ran for the Senate in 1941 in another special election, his wife accompanied him on the campaign trail and filmed home movies that recorded the pageantry of her husband's well-financed canvass. Despite both enthusiastic support from Pres. Franklin D. Roosevelt and a statewide effort, Lyndon lost narrowly to the state's popular chief executive, Gov. W. Lee "Pass the Biscuits, Pappy" O'Daniel. The Johnsons returned to Washington in autumn 1941 and soon found their lives overtaken by the march of impending war. Shortly after Pearl Harbor, Lyndon Johnson went on active duty as a naval reserve officer. In the next several months, the congressman lobbied for an assignment in the war zone while his wife assisted with the operation of his Washington office. By late April 1942, Commander Johnson was on his way to the South Pacific.

Lady Bird Johnson took over the work in Congress that her husband had left. "The office is so stimulating and interesting," she wrote on 3 March, "that I 'graduated myself' from business school and now get down here about eight-thirty every morning and stay until Lyndon Johnson quitting time—which is when everything is done." She dealt with an array of problems—the status of the city slaughterhouse in Austin, the location of an Army Air Support

Command there, and the impact of rationing and housing problems in the district. Always there were the lists of people to write, congratulating them on weddings, graduations, or local honors and, in regard to the war, providing news about heroism, wounds, and death. During these months, Lady Bird Johnson received a political education. She wrote to a friend that she had learned more in those three months than in her four years in college. Looking back on the whole experience, she recalled, "It gave me a sense of, sort of reassurance about myself because I finally emerged thinking that — well, I could make a living for myself." [27]

During these months, Mrs. Johnson was involved in deciding whether her husband should enter the Senate primary against O'Daniel, who was then seeking a full six-year term. Her judgment was that Lyndon should opt for reelection to the House because it was unlikely that he would defeat the popular O'Daniel. Other friends of Johnson's agreed, and they helped her secure the petitions that put the congressman on the primary ballot without opposition. By mid-July, Johnson had returned from the South Pacific on what his wife then described as "the grandest day of my life." [28]

After Lyndon's homecoming, she persuaded him that they should use money that she was receiving from her inheritance to buy a house in Washington. She located a two-story, eight-room colonial house in the northwest part of the city near Connecticut Avenue. Finally, she would have enough room to live and a garden for her outdoor passions. When he imperiled the sale by dickering about the price, she erupted before a startled Lyndon and John B. Connally Jr.: "I want that house! Every woman wants a home of her own. I've lived out of a suitcase ever since we've been married. I have no home to look forward to. I have no children to look forward to and I have nothing to look forward to but another election." As she left the room, a bewildered Johnson asked Connally, "What should I do?" Connally's terse answer: "I'd buy the house." [29]

Once the new home was acquired, she turned with particular pleasure to the yard and garden. "The sunshine was so inviting," she wrote to friends in March 1943, "that I spent a couple of more enthusiastic than useful hours digging in my flower garden." Eventually the garden became "quite a remarkable" one, "about 30 by 30 in the backyard of my little house," where she raised zinnias and peonies.

As she drove back and forth between Washington and Texas in the prewar years and later after the war ended, she also marked the changes in the landscape; the junkyards, the billboards, and the impact of development on natural beauty. Nonetheless, "I loved the trips across the country to Washington," she later said, "and I never got too many of them."[30]

By spring 1943, however, Lady Bird Johnson had begun another project. The Johnsons had bought radio station KTBC in Austin, from which grew an extensive investment in radio and television stations in Texas over the next twenty years. The impulse that prompted the Johnsons into this new venture arose from the uncertainties of politics. "Both Lyndon and I were interested in having a little piece of the communications world," she said, and they explored the possibility of acquiring a country newspaper in East Texas. Then the opportunity arose to purchase the Austin station. "I had a degree in journalism and we knew a lot of folks in the business. It just held an attraction for us, and we thought it was a coming industry."[31]

The place of KTBC and other media holdings in the life of the Johnsons remains controversial and murky because their corporate records are still closed. Clearly, Lyndon Johnson wielded his political influence with networks and advertisers to make his radio and television stations profitable. During the 1960s it was widely believed in Washington that "the Senate Majority Leader could make a success of a television station in the Gobi Desert." Johnson knew precisely how to exert pressure in order to produce advertising revenues. Sponsors found it advantageous, for example, to buy time on Johnson's radio station, even though the size of the Austin market, in comparison to other cities, was still relatively modest.[32]

Lady Bird Johnson played a significant role in the acquisition of the station and its day-to-day operations thereafter. Her inheritance was crucial in providing the money to acquire KTBC in January 1943. Her uncle, Claude Patillo, put in about $40,000, and Aunt Effie loaned her another $40,500. From that total, she paid for a house in Austin, the house in Washington, and the $17,500 that was required to purchase KTBC. Her application to the Federal Communications Commission (FCC) listed her net worth at $64,322, and a supporting document said that "she has recently served approximately a year as secretary for the Congressman." Once the purchase was made, the Johnsons still had to make a success of what one employee described as "a very run-down station."[33]

Lyndon told his wife, "You have to go down there and take that place over." When she walked into the station, two blocks off Congress Avenue, she found "that the place was *real* dirty. I mean cobwebs on the windows and the floor was grimy." Employees remembered that she scrubbed the floor herself. More important, she brought in new staff members to revitalize the operation. She set about paying off old bills and working through the accounts receivable. The station was in the red during the first half of 1943, but her efforts enabled it to be "in the black in August to the tune of eighteen dollars." From then on the station was consistently profitable, especially in the postwar years when the area began its population growth.[34]

The key to the station's initial success was Mrs. Johnson's ability to persuade the FCC to grant KTBC the right to broadcast twenty-four hours a day and to increase its transmitting power to 1,000 watts. She also obtained network affiliation with the Columbia Broadcasting System, given the help of Lyndon's friendship with the network's president William S. Paley. Mrs. Johnson received detailed weekly reports about the station's progress, along with monthly budgets, when she was in Washington. Associates said that, on the business side, she was "any man's equal; she reads a balance sheet like most women examine a piece of cloth." When she moved into the White House and had to transfer her interest in the station and other media properties to a trust, she wrote of her nostalgia about ending her formal connection with KTBC: "Trading in a twenty-two-year love and work for the months that lie ahead brought a torrent of thoughts and emotions in its wake. . . . How I shall miss the plans, the people—even the problems—the affiliates conventions, yes, even the thick Saturday morning reports, the Christmas party, and perhaps even more, the summer parties with everybody's children."[35]

By 1952 the Johnsons had applied for a television-station license in Austin, and their application showed that KTBC was worth almost $.5 million. The FCC granted the license, and the new station enjoyed a monopoly of television coverage in the Austin area for more than a decade. During this same period the holdings of the Johnsons included stations in Waco and Corpus Christi as well as other properties in land and businesses in the Austin area amounting to more than $10 million. Lyndon's political clout was an indispensable element in the growth of their business empire, but so too was Lady Bird Johnson's entrepreneurial talents.

During the first decade of their marriage, the Johnsons tried unsuccessfully to have children. Then in March 1944 their first daughter was born. "I wanted to name her Lady Bird," Lyndon told one of his friends, "but her mother preferred Lynda Bird, and since she is the boss I had to compromise." Mrs. Johnson was reported to be seriously ill during summer 1945, and she lost a baby because of a tubal pregnancy in 1946. A year later, however, in July 1947, the Johnsons had their second daughter, Lucy Baines Johnson.[36]

The two girls grew up in a household that was an extension of their parents' political lives. Mrs. Johnson employed Helen Williams to run the house when she was absent, and such staff members as Mary Rather and Willie Day Taylor came over from the House and later the Senate offices to assist with the children. Lynda and Luci took readily to their semicelebrity status. They became close friends with Speaker Sam Rayburn, who often attended their birthday parties. Lady Bird Johnson's daughters understood that their parents loved them but that these family ties existed within the context of their father's political ambitions and their mother's business and social priorities.

During the latter part of the 1940s, Lady Bird Johnson also became more centrally involved with her husband's political career. Hardy Hollers, Lyndon's opponent in the 1946 Democratic primary campaign for the House, attacked the Johnsons' family finances and alleged that the congressman and his wife had profited from his public service. So bitter did the contest become that the Johnson camp debated whether Mrs. Johnson should answer the charges in her own radio address. In the end, the speech was not given, and Johnson easily defeated Hollers. The episode began the public questioning about the Johnsons' fortune and his personal ethics that lasted through Lyndon's presidency.

Two years later, when Lyndon Johnson faced Coke Stevenson in the bitter Democratic primary campaign for U.S. senator, Mrs.

Johnson was a prominent force in the campaign. She helped orga-
nize the Women's Division, and she toured the state with her associate, Marietta Brooks, talking to groups of women. One newspaper
called Lady Bird Johnson "an able vote getter," though the reporter
found her "a rather modest woman" who "used to even be on the shy
side." Johnson and Stevenson met in the August runoff, Johnson still
trying to eat away at the former governor's lead. The night before
the voting, Lady Bird rode to San Antonio to join Lyndon. Her car
was in two accidents, but despite the resulting bruises, she went on
to San Antonio, "made a fine speech," and then returned to Austin
where she telephoned voters throughout election day. The results
gave Johnson a controversial and contested eighty-seven-vote victory, which kept them in court and in suspense until the new senator
took the oath in January 1949. "The 1948 campaign was one that just
didn't end," Lady Bird Johnson later said; "it just went on and on." [37]

After Lyndon's election to the Senate, the Johnsons purchased
land on the Pedernales River between Johnson City and Freder-
icksburg in the Hill Country. The property was acquired from the
senator's aunt and was in run-down condition. Lady Bird Johnson
was not prepared for the move from Austin and had a reaction of
"complete withdrawal" when she saw the place. "I was aghast! How
can you *possibly* do this to me?" she asked him. In the end her husband's enthusiasm and the pull of the Hill Country overcame her
qualms. "I gradually began to get wrapped up in it myself. I have
always loved living on the land. It was just that I had grown up in
such a completely different sort of land." [38]

While redecorating the inside of what would become the LBJ
Ranch, she also spread seventy-five pounds of bluebonnet seeds on
both sides of the river. And she worked with seed dealers to place
other wildflowers across the property. As the 1950s unfolded, the
ranch became a place for their political guests, entertainment, and
"a good visit" with friends from everywhere. In a sense the LBJ
Ranch was the first example of Lady Bird Johnson's skill at beautifying the landscape. [39]

In July 1955, Lyndon Johnson suffered a serious heart attack. A
heavy smoker, he drove himself hard, ate irregularly, and had put
on forty extra pounds. A local doctor told him in late June: "Lyndon
you're too fat; you're going to have a heart attack." On 2 July, while

driving to the home of his friend and political patron George Brown in Virginia, Lyndon experienced severe chest pains, which doctors quickly diagnosed as a heart attack. Lady Bird received a phone call: "Lyndon's on his way to Bethesda Naval Hospital in an ambulance. Our local doctor thinks it may be a heart attack." She was at the hospital when he arrived, and he said, "And you stay here. I'd rather fight with you beside me. I'm sure we'll lick this." She remained at the hospital until he was released five weeks later. As he recovered, Lady Bird Johnson grappled with "the difficulties of breaking the smoking habit and going on this dismal low-calorie/low-fat diet." Lyndon got his weight back down to 180 pounds, and in the process she dropped fourteen pounds herself.[40]

Other changes in his lifestyle proved more difficult. "My husband was always a taut, driving perfectionist who lived with constant tension," she said in 1956; she hoped that the needed rest might turn his mind toward diversions and relaxations. Her hopes were disappointed. As she remarked to one friend in a moment of candor, Lyndon "has no natural cultural bent." The heart attack did not change his intellectual habits, but it did alter their mutual sensitivity about his health. As the diary she kept during the presidency indicates, she was conscious of his medical condition and vigilant about it throughout the rest of their life together.[41]

By early 1956 a recovered Lyndon had resumed his Senate duties and had begun to be talked about as a presidential or vice-presidential hopeful. At the Democratic National Convention in August 1956 he made an abortive attempt to derail the candidacy of Adlai Stevenson. Mrs. Johnson laughed when reporters asked her how she would feel about being First Lady. "That's a long way into the distant future in that vast convention of folks," she responded. She was equally skeptical about her husband's chances against Stevenson: "I no more expect it to happen than I do to walk out that door and have lightning strike me." [42]

Nineteen fifty-six was not Johnson's year, but the prospect of national office and future campaigning for the couple was more likely as the decade ended. Still shy about appearing before an audience, Lady Bird Johnson enrolled in a formal public-speaking course at the Capitol Speakers Club in 1959. The experience relieved some of her anxieties about delivering speeches as she learned to talk more slowly and to pitch her voice lower. By spring 1960 she was able to introduce her husband to a women's conference as "an exciting man to live with; an exhausting man to keep up with; a man who has worn well in the twenty-five years we have been together." Speaking still made her nervous, and "her hands shook so she could barely hold her speech notes" before a campaign appearance in October 1960. Continued practice and her own determination, however, enabled her to develop a comfortable and effective style of public speaking by the time she came to the White House in 1963.[43]

In 1960 Lyndon Johnson made a more serious and sustained run for the presidency. Mrs. Johnson prepared to campaign for him and to set up a women's organization for his drive for the nomination. The senator waited until just before the Democratic National Convention in July 1960 to announce his candidacy formally. His passivity, which allowed John F. Kennedy to build up a large lead in delegates, may have stemmed from personal reasons as much as from a strategy of emphasizing the demands of his Senate duties and avoiding the primaries. Aides later recalled his infatuation with a woman who was working in his office and intimated that he had considered breaking up his marriage. In any case, the majority leader's indecisive course limited his wife to making occasional public comments about him before the party assembled in Los Angeles. Johnson's candidacy then went down to defeat before the better-organized and nationally based Kennedy campaign on the first ballot. Lady Bird Johnson told reporters that although "Lyndon would have made a noble president," she had "a sizable feeling of relief" at the result.[44]

The events of the next two days, which involved Johnson's being selected as Kennedy's running mate, saw Lady Bird Johnson as an active participant. She took the first phone call from Kennedy on Thursday morning, 14 July, when he asked for a meeting with her husband. "I know he's going to offer the vice-presidency, and I hope you won't take it," she said. Mrs. Johnson was there when Philip Graham, publisher of the *Washington Post,* arrived. "Lady Bird tried to leave," Graham recalled in a famous memorandum, but "Johnson and I lunged after her, saying she was needed on this one." She advised Lyndon not to see Robert F. Kennedy, who was then talking in another room with Sam Rayburn; she warned him to speak only to the nominee. When the confusion worked itself out and Johnson finally made a statement to the press that he would accept the second spot on the ticket, he and his wife stood there, in Graham's words, "looking as though they had just survived an airplane crash." After Lyndon had become the vice-presidential choice, his wife stated the alternatives he had faced with her characteristic lucidity: "It was not a spot he would have sought; he had just not thought about it, but the way it was put to him — that the Party needed him — struck a responsive chord."[45]

In the ensuing campaign, Lady Bird Johnson was the most visible woman that the Democrats put before the voters. Jacqueline Kennedy was pregnant and little disposed to conduct an active campaign. Mrs. Johnson announced her plans to tour Texas in late August with Eunice Shriver (Kennedy's sister) and Ethel Kennedy (Robert Kennedy's wife). When a questioner at the press conference raised the issue of opposition to Kennedy's Catholicism in Texas, Mrs. Johnson replied: "There is such a thing as a religious issue. That we all know. But the more deeply one reads the Bible, the more fair one is going to be. And so, I do not believe it will be a decisive issue in our state." She also deftly answered a reporter's probe about medical care for the elderly. Her father's private resources had enabled him to afford nursing care that an eighty-six-year-old man required; people without that advantage would confront "financial ruin" when illness came. To another inquiry about Mrs. Kennedy's hairstyle, her crisp response was, "I think it's more important what's inside the head than what's outside."[46]

Lady Bird Johnson emerged as a major force in the Democratic effort in 1960. The wife of the vice-presidential candidate became central in the appeal to southern voters, whose Democratic allegiance had slipped during the Eisenhower years. She crisscrossed the region in tours that represented the largest part of the 35,000 miles she traveled in all. "Campaigning would be tiring, if it weren't so much fun," she said in Charlotte, North Carolina. She urged voters in Corpus Christi, Texas, to do "five things" for her husband and the Democrats: "He wants you to write a card to all your kinfolks, have a coffee or tea party for your friends, phone ten people and ask each of them to phone ten more, write a letter to the editor of your newspaper, and drive a full car to the polls on November eighth." Campaigning in a red dress, she used chartered planes to reach the rallies, but she was most in her element on the whistle-stop tours of "cold hot cakes and early sunrises" through Alabama and the Deep South. When she traveled with Lyndon, she reminded him if he was speaking too long, and she mended his split pants in Albuquerque after he rode a horse in a parade.[47]

Two events punctuated the campaign. First, T. J. Taylor, who had been ill for some time, began to fail in late September, and Mrs. Johnson interrupted her schedule to go to Marshall. Three weeks later his condition again worsened, and she returned to the hospital. He died on 22 October. After the funeral, she returned to the hustings, but she retained a keen interest in her hometown, her father's house, and the life he had made in Karnack.

The second event occurred four days before the voting. The Johnsons were to address a luncheon of Democrats at the Adolphus Hotel in Dallas. As their motorcade reached the downtown area, it encountered several thousand enthusiastic Republican partisans who had just seen Richard M. Nixon off at the airport. The sign-waving crowd forced the Johnsons to leave their car at the Baker Hotel, on the other side of Commerce Street. Inside the Baker the sound of the chanting mob could still be heard, and the couple decided that they had to go back across to the Adolphus, lest the Republicans claim success for their intimidating tactics.

It was a difficult moment. As they moved into the throng, Mrs. Johnson was spit upon, and one member of the crowd hit her with a sign. "I just had to keep on walking and suppress all emotions," she recalled, "and be just like Marie Antoinette in the tumbrel." One witness said that Lady Bird Johnson nearly lost her temper and tried to answer one of the "young, Junior League types," but Lyndon "put his hand over her mouth and stopped that and brought her right along." His height enabled him to see above the crowd; "she could only see up." The episode backfired on the Republicans and may have added to the narrow victory that put Texas in the Democratic column. Robert F. Kennedy put Mrs. Johnson's contributions to the campaign in a larger context, in a way that also diminished her husband's role on the ticket: "Lady Bird carried Texas for us."[48]

The three years that Lady Bird Johnson (then the Second Lady) spent as the wife of the vice-president proved to be a useful preparation for the duties she assumed in November 1963. Her goal was "helping Lyndon all I can, helping Mrs. Kennedy whenever she needs me, and becoming a more alive me." Jacqueline Kennedy treated the ceremonial duties of a president's wife as burdens that she discharged when it suited her. As a result, Lady Bird Johnson became, as one journalist said, "Washington's No. 1 pinch hitter." She greeted women delegates from the United Nations in December 1961, accepted an Emmy award for Mrs. Kennedy in May 1962, and stood in for her in April 1963 at a luncheon of the Senate Ladies Red Cross group. "I don't know how we could get along without Lady Bird," said one White House aide during these years.[49]

To meet the increased responsibilities of the vice-presidency, the Johnsons moved into a larger house that they had purchased from the perennial Washington hostess Perle Mesta (the vice-president had no official residence in those days). The Elms' had sufficient space for entertaining and an office for Mrs. Johnson. She also acquired the beginnings of a personal staff. Bess Abell, the daughter of Sen. Earle Clements of Kentucky, was her secretary, and Elizabeth "Liz" Carpenter handled her press relations. The two women made an effective team. Abell was quiet and understated, with a dry wit and a close knowledge of the Washington scene. Carpenter, a graduate of the University of Texas, supplied an infectious ebullience that endeared her to the reporters who covered Lady Bird Johnson. She also understood, from her own days as a Washington journalist, about deadlines, access, and candor.[50]

As vice-president, Lyndon Johnson traveled extensively, and the trips the couple made provided Mrs. Johnson with an impressive exposure to new cultural and public experiences. They went to Senegal in April 1961; and in her account of the trip, she picked out as the symbol of that African nation "the strange but fascinating baobob tree which stands sturdily over all the landscape and in the lives of the people." That same spring the Johnsons traveled to six Asian nations, and the flowers that she saw remained a vivid memory. "Exquisite orange trees full of blossoms greeted us first at Hawaii and kept appearing along the way; only when we got to Pakistan, with the countryside and climate not unlike Texas, did the lowly zinnia and petunia show up." Other trips included a tour of the Mediterranean and the Middle East in late summer 1962 and a final trip to Scandinavia in September 1963. "We tromped through the forests of Sweden and Finland, picking lingonberries," Mrs. Johnson reported.[51]

At home, Lady Bird Johnson was finding her own voice and role in Washington. She concluded that "American women are under-going a great revolution in our lifetime. We have learned to master dishwashers, typewriters, and voting machines with reasonable aplomb. We must now try to make our laws catch up with what has happened to us as we bounce in and out of the labor market and raise a family." In the pocket notebook that she carried during those years, "I make little lists and scratch 'em off"; she moved through days including activities as varied as a visit to a Peace Corps Center in Oklahoma, a ground-breaking ceremony for a public-works facility in West Virginia, and the Spanish lessons she was taking.[52]

Gradually the public realized that the vice-president's wife was a singular individual. The chairman of the Indiana Public Service Commission, publicly announcing his criteria for a secretary, included "the charm of Lady Bird Johnson" among his desired specifications. The *Washington Post* called her "a lady of exceptional grace" who had rendered "unstinting and indefatigable public service." As fall 1963 began, she told columnist Ruth Montgomery that she relished her role as the vice-president's wife. "I'd be a vegetable if I didn't! I have an omnivorous curiosity about the wide, wide world, and Lyndon's position has given me an unparalleled opportunity to be exposed to it both at home and abroad."[53]

The woman who was preparing to welcome President and Mrs. Kennedy to the LBJ Ranch in November 1963 had come a long distance from the little girl who had walked in the forest near Caddo Lake four decades earlier. Through the years of college and early marriage, motherhood and political campaigns, business and notoriety, she had maintained her own identity against what Anne Morrow Lindbergh called, in a phrase that Lady Bird Johnson quoted, "the fragmentation of self." Her husband rarely read books, but she was bookish, almost intellectual. He had no time for the theater; she loved Broadway and saw plays alone in Washington. Lyndon's volatility made working for him alternately a stimulus and an ordeal. Her calmness soothed pained feelings and eased the hurts he inflicted. They were a team of strong individuals, and they were about to join the ranks of the most famous people in the world.[54]

CHAPTER 2

BECOMING FIRST LADY

Lady Bird Johnson became First Lady on 22 November 1963, but the events of that day were so traumatic that it took her some months to evolve her own style in the White House. "Oh, Mrs. Kennedy," she said on the plane that flew back from Dallas, "you know we never even wanted to be vice-president and now, dear God, it's come to this." In her diary, Mrs. Johnson wrote later, "I would have done anything to help her, but there was nothing I could do, so rather quickly I left and went back to the main part of the airplane where everyone was seated." The painful transition to the role of First Lady left her momentarily shaken. "I feel as if I am suddenly on stage for a part I never rehearsed," she told a friend.[1]

In the early weeks of Lyndon Johnson's presidency, there was much for Lady Bird Johnson to do. She had to sell the Elms, put their television interests in a blind trust, and seek advice on how to function as the First Lady. As she wrote in her diary for 26 November 1963, "Now the time has come to get the wheels of life rolling again." Liz Carpenter became the director of Mrs. Johnson's staff and the first officially designated press secretary to the First Lady. Bess Abell continued as the social secretary.[2]

The appointment of Carpenter, a Washington newswoman, underscored Mrs. Johnson's perception that press relations would be central to her success. It was "a whole new adjustment for me —

having every move watched and covered and considered news." But she adapted readily to the presence of reporters and the trappings of celebrity that accompanied being First Lady. Mrs. Johnson also knew about the growing influence of television. Network news programs had expanded from fifteen minutes to half an hour in autumn 1963, and their cameras and crews were more visible presences in the White House scene as coverage of the presidency increased during the early 1960s. Simone Poulain joined Liz Carpenter's staff to manage the First Lady's relations with television.[3]

Handling the female press corps in the White House required further adjustments. Mrs. Johnson met with these women on 10 January 1964 for tea, "to set the tenor of press conferences — not as conferences but informal meetings — as an invitation to a relaxed and pleasant atmosphere with an opportunity to meet somebody else who was newsworthy." Like her immediate predecessors, Lady Bird Johnson did not intend to emulate the regularly held press conferences that had been Eleanor Roosevelt's trademark as First Lady. Instead, she had developed an approach consisting of luncheons for "Women Doers" during the vice-presidential years. It offered her a way of recognizing prominent and successful women while providing them with a platform for their ideas. Since it was a semisocial occasion, it allowed the First Lady and her staff a degree of control over the agenda and questions. The technique became a staple of her White House days. Guests heard an active woman discuss public questions with one or more journalists present but without the freewheeling atmosphere of a press conference.[4]

Lady Bird Johnson enjoyed a good press from her earliest days in the White House. Unlike her husband, she paid little attention to what was written about her and conducted no vendettas against reporters whom she disliked. Journalist Nan Robertson once remarked that Mrs. Johnson had "an instinctive sense of public relations polished during nearly twenty-eight years of public life. . . . She is sympathetic to reporters' problems and needs." Some of this skill stemmed from her journalistic background. "She knew the language of the trade," Liz Carpenter recalled, "the difference between an A.M. and P.M. deadline, that it is better to be accessible than evasive." Moreover, the frequent trips that she made created a rapport with the newswomen who accompanied her.[5]

Lady Bird Johnson watches as Lyndon Johnson takes the oath of office on
22 November 1963. (White House photo by Cecil Stoughton, LBJ Library)

At this time Lady Bird Johnson decided to create a formal record of her time near the presidency. The diary that she began keeping in late November 1963 eventually reached nearly 1.75 million words. Sometimes on the same day, sometimes a day or a week later, she would sit down with files and clippings that were designed to prod her memory and dictate her recollections into a tape recorder. Most of the recording occurred "in a small room in the southwest corner of the second floor of the White House." A sign on the door said, "I want to be alone."[6]

In 1970, one-seventh of Lady Bird Johnson's diary was published as *A White House Diary*. Though there are gaps, and some subjects, such as beautification, are only sporadically covered, the *Diary* is a valuable record of what the First Lady did and how she operated in the White House. It is the most complete account of its kind by a presidential wife, and it offers insights into her husband's character that remain valuable.

While Lady Bird Johnson served as an advocate for programs

Lady Bird Johnson and Liz Carpenter, 19 May 1964.
(LBJ Library photograph, 32428)

and as a presidential partner, she was also the mother of two young women who came under the same media glare that their parents experienced. Lynda Bird Johnson was nineteen when her father became president. She was attending the University of Texas and majoring in history, as her mother had done. Tall and straight like her father, Lynda had a rapid-fire intelligence and a dry, understated wit. During the 1960s she had not yet blossomed into the attractive woman she would become. Her father said, with mingled pride and unconscious chauvinism, "Lynda Bird is so smart that she will always be able to make a living for herself." At the White House she took full advantage of the opportunities to meet the famous and the celebrated, including the movie actor George Hamilton. She married Charles S. Robb, a Marine officer, in 1967.[7]

In 1963 Lucy Baines Johnson (she became Luci during the presidency) was an exuberant, outgoing sixteen-year-old, who seemed, on the surface, a teenager of the 1960s. Her father believed that she was "so appealing and feminine there will always be some man around wanting to make a living for her." In 1966 she married Patrick J. Nugent of Wisconsin. Luci's energy and flair made her a media favorite. She also had a serious side, which her mother and father saw. Personal searching led to her conversion to Catholicism, and her marriage encountered internal stresses that foreshadowed her subsequent divorce.[8]

Lady Bird Johnson's most important commitment was to her husband. She poured into her diary her worries about her husband's health and his personal sense of well-being. She feared that Lyndon might end up like Woodrow Wilson, his health broken by the cares of office. "I wish we could do something about these sleepless nights," she wrote in 1966. In November 1982 she told students at the University of Texas how much she disliked the pile of reading that appeared on the president's pillow each evening and how pleased she felt when there was only a small amount for her husband to do.[9]

On her own, she kept track of the issues and problems of the presidency. When she traveled, she received briefings from the White House staff, including its senior members, about such issues as nuclear policy and the economy. She gave advice about diplomatic appointments and was deeply involved in literacy and the fate of the Head Start program. Like her husband, she expressed an

*Postcard of the First Family, showing the president, Mrs. Johnson, and their
daughters. (author's collection)*

interest in population-control questions. When she talked about the
possibility of sending a supportive telegram to Planned Parenthood
in early 1965, White House aide Horace Busby warned Liz Carpenter that such a gesture might be misconstrued "as the signal for a
family crusade, Eleanor Roosevelt style." The telegram was not sent.
In addition to her concern for beautification, Mrs. Johnson showed
a detailed grasp of other environmental matters.[10]

During the early years of his presidency, when Lyndon Johnson endeavored to enhance the role of women in the administration, his wife applauded his efforts. "Next to cutting out waste in government," she said in a speech to the Kentucky Federation of Women's Clubs in May 1964, "finding jobs for competent women is Lyndon's daily delight." In 1967, when the discussions were occurring about who should replace retiring justice Tom Clark on the Supreme Court, the president discussed possible African American nominees and wondered whether he should appoint the first woman to the Court. Presidential aide Joseph Califano recalled that "rare for her, Lady Bird broke in. She thought that 'Lyndon had done so much' for blacks, 'why not indeed fill the vacancy with a woman.'" In the end the president decided to select Thurgood Marshall.[11]

In many respects, she was her husband's closest adviser. As the years progressed, the Johnsons talked often "in the early hours of the morning." She was an important contributor to his speeches. She provided a draft proposal regarding the seating of the Mississippi delegation in 1964, which recommended in favor of the white Democrats and against the Freedom Democratic party. In 1966 she read the "final draft of the domestic part" of the State of the Union speech and "suggested a little sentence about thrift and common sense in the conduct of the war on poverty, with due respect for spending the tax payer's dollar."[12]

She was a candid critic, and the president accepted changes from her that no other adviser could have proposed. Early in the presidency, she critiqued one of his televised speeches, always a sore point with Lyndon Johnson: he hated the medium and its unflattering portrayal of his character. "You want to listen for about one minute to my critique?" she asked on 7 March 1964; "or would you rather wait until tonight?" When Lyndon agreed to hear what she had to say, she told him, "You were a little breathless and there was too much looking down and I think it was a little too fast. Not enough change of pace." Summing up, she told him, "In general, I'd say it was a good B-plus." The president accepted her measured evaluation with a good grace he would not have chosen to display to any of his subordinates.[13]

Throughout the White House years she identified with the goals of her husband's administration and hoped for its success. The

Johnsons had their disagreements over issues and strategy, and he teased her publicly and privately about her beautification campaign. But she remained the one person in whom he confided with complete trust because she had, in Wilbur Cohen's words, "no ulterior purpose." Her influence was large, and her part in his administration was important. "He trusted her advice and judgment," said his aide Harry McPherson. And as Hubert H. Humphrey noted, "In her quiet way, she made him come to heel." Their friend and the Austin wit, Richard "Cactus" Pryor, said wryly: "No telling how many crises have been avoided by Lady Bird Johnson saying to her husband: 'Now, Lyndon.' "[14]

Beyond her duties as mother, wife, and political partner lay the question of what her role as First Lady should be. Friends and the writers of early articles about her assured the public that she would find important things to do. Katie Louchheim wrote that Mrs. Johnson was "by disposition, experience, and inclination what President Johnson calls a 'can-do' woman" and predicted that the First Lady would consider ways in which "she might make the White House a showcase for women of achievement." Columnist Ruth Montgomery wrote that "Lady Bird is still growing," citing friends who forecast "that she will one day take her place as one of America's great First Ladies."[15]

The institution of presidential wife had evolved greatly from the passivity and reclusiveness that marked White House spouses during the nineteenth century. During the first thirty years of the twentieth century, First Ladies had gradually become more active and more visible on the Washington social scene. Some of them, such as Edith Roosevelt and Grace Coolidge, had been cultural and social leaders of Washington, the former holding musicales at the White House. Other wives had been important influences on their husbands, beyond the public's gaze. Before her crippling illness in spring 1909, Helen Herron Taft had pushed her husband's presidential candidacy, advised him on appointments, and consulted about his legislative program. Edith Bolling Wilson had taken on quasi-presidential duties when Woodrow Wilson's stroke disabled him between October 1919 and March 1921. These women had assumed some of the attributes of celebrities as popular interest in the First Lady and the family of the president quickened after 1900.

In the early 1930s, Eleanor Roosevelt transformed the role of the First Lady into a combination of ombudswoman to the nation, an advocate for the disadvantaged, and an agent of the president. She used her fame and influence to stretch the boundaries of the New Deal in her commitment to black Americans, the young, and the less privileged. As the wife of a congressman between 1937 and 1945, Lady Bird Johnson saw Eleanor Roosevelt and felt an empathy for her that never diminished. "I had an awful lot of respect for her hard work, and her caring, and her knowledge," Mrs. Johnson said, though she told the same interviewer that she had similar feelings about Dolley Todd Madison and Abigail Smith Adams. Mrs. Johnson once walked the alleys of Washington with Mrs. Roosevelt, and she saw the First Lady attend a benefit luncheon in 1939 at which only one person could be helped. "But where else do you start except with one person?" Mrs. Johnson asked when she spoke about the occasion in April 1964.[16]

Lady Bird Johnson was astute enough to recognize, however, that Eleanor Roosevelt's independent style had often brought political difficulties for her husband. Moreover, Mrs. Roosevelt's ample energies had been diffused into too many causes and too much activity, as her fame became a substitute for a clear focus on which priorities to pursue. A First Lady in the Eleanor Roosevelt vein would have to find a direction for activism that gave her programs coherence and political appeal.

After Eleanor Roosevelt's tenure, the institution of the First Lady had receded from the high point of public interest. Bess Wallace Truman deliberately made herself a retiring contrast to her predecessor while exercising a good deal of influence behind the scenes. Mamie Doud Eisenhower had no ambitions to sway her husband on substantive questions, and a chronic illness limited her commitments while she was in the White House. "She was very much against pushing forward into public view," Dwight D. Eisenhower said after he left the presidency.[17]

The three years that Jacqueline Kennedy spent as First Lady revitalized the institution and made the wife of the president a figure of glamour and sophistication. The legacy that Mrs. Kennedy left to her successor was an image of beauty, culture, and good taste that no other woman could easily attain. As a high school history

teacher in Maine said of Mrs. Johnson in 1967, "What she suf-
fers from is having had to follow a goddess." There were memories
of the dazzling parties and the artistic occasions where President
and Mrs. Kennedy had enthralled their guests. Her sponsoring the
restoration and renewal of the mansion in the style of the early-
nineteenth-century United States enhanced the image of gentility
and elegance that she conveyed. Lady Bird Johnson liked and admired Jacqueline Kennedy and felt deeply for her in her grief. They
remained friends until Mrs. Kennedy's death in 1994.[18]

If Lady Bird Johnson knew about the less happy side of Jacqueline
Kennedy's years as First Lady, she never mentioned such facts publicly or privately. Early in her diary, Mrs. Johnson noted that Mrs.
Kennedy achieved on the day of her husband's funeral "something
she had never quite achieved in the years she'd been in the White
House—a state of love, a state of rapport between herself and the
people of this country." There was more ambivalence about Mrs.
Kennedy's approach to her duties in the 1960s than would be apparent four decades later.[19]

When it suited her, Mrs. Kennedy could be visible and seemingly
accessible. But if she chafed at the ceremonial duties of the president's wife, then she simply did not do them; and she often relied on
Lady Bird Johnson to act in her stead. Beyond the restoration of the
White House and a general appreciation of the arts, Mrs. Kennedy
pursued no programs and mobilized no constituencies. She disliked
politics in the first place, but her stance also kept her at a distance
from a husband whose chronic womanizing continued even when
he was president. These aspects of Mrs. Kennedy's life, however,
were not available to Lady Bird Johnson as guides to her own conduct or as reasons for her to follow a different path as First Lady. She
had to be herself, but she had to do it in ways that would not cast
even an implied rebuke on the woman who had preceded her.

Lady Bird Johnson began to evolve her own style as First Lady in
mid-January 1964 with her initial trip on behalf of the president and
his "unconditional war on poverty" that he had declared in his State
of the Union message. She went to coal-mining regions of Pennsylvania, which she labeled "the first battleground" of that war. For
her, "it was a day I loved living," composed of "a montage of faces,
outstretched hands in the biting cold, children wanting autographs,

roses." Other well-organized trips followed during her career as
First Lady, as the nation got to know her. At the end of January, *U.S.
News and World Report* observed that "Lady Bird Johnson is setting
a pace as First Lady that hasn't been matched since Eleanor Roosevelt's day." [20]

In the ensuing months, Lady Bird Johnson kept up the same busy
schedule. She traveled to Huntsville, Alabama, to visit the Space
Flight Center in late March, where she told the audience that "the
South has hitched its wagon to the stars." She went with the president in April on a five-state swing that included the Appalachian
region of Kentucky. She returned the next month to the "beautiful
but economically depressed Cumberland Plateau of the same state."
Finally, she delivered the baccalaureate address at Radcliffe College
in early June. It was a speech "that I had worked on harder than any
other." She told the women graduates: "If you achieve the precious
balance between women's domestic and civic life, you can do more
for zest and sanity in our society than by any other achievement." [21]

During 1964 she espoused a mild, cautious feminism as she
searched for a theme to guide her years in the White House. In the
Radcliffe address, she said that "a quite remarkable young woman
has been emerging in the United States, she might be called the
natural woman, the complete woman." The First Lady added that
this new woman did not "want to be the long-striding feminist in
low heels, engaged in a conscious war with men," but hoped to become "preeminently a woman, wife, a mother, a thinking citizen."
She maintained that American women held "a tremendous potential of strength for good" when they exerted their forces as "we mark
a ballot, teach our children, or work for a better community." [22]

For the most part, the general public response to Lady Bird Johnson during these early months was positive. Republican congressmen went to Alabama in the spring, however, and found black ten-
ant farmers living in poverty on the land that the First Lady owned
in that state. The implied contrast between the War on Poverty and
the squalid state of the tenants made political points, as President
Johnson well recognized. In one of his recorded telephone calls, the
president called it "just pure cheap politics," and the episode did
not have any lasting impact. Otherwise, the First Lady drew friendly
crowds and admiring reviews. Biographies appeared that brought a

sense of her life and style to the public. "You're doing a wonderful job. Everybody says so," Robert F. Kennedy told her at Gen. Douglas MacArthur's funeral in April.[23]

She had not yet solved the problem of what program she would pursue in the White House. The Women Doers luncheons provided a means to put talented women before the press corps, but these gatherings by themselves did not constitute a coherent agenda. She carried forward some of the restoration work that Mrs. Kennedy had begun. Working with Washington attorney Clark Clifford, she proceeded with the creation of the office of Curator of the White House and the establishment of a Committee for the Preservation of the White House. Mrs. Johnson also helped Mrs. Paul Mellon bring to completion her plans to rename the East Garden the Jacqueline Kennedy Garden.

In a halting and tentative way in 1964, she began to focus on the idea that became beautification. In February of that year the Cincinnati Park Commission wrote to the president about planting a tree in his honor in that city's Eden Park. "The President has turned your letter over to me," Mrs. Johnson replied, "because I am more of a gardener than he is." She suggested a live oak that would be "close to my husband's boyhood." Later in the summer, at the suggestion of Secretary of the Interior Stewart Udall, she opened the American Landmarks Celebration on the garden steps of Woodrow Wilson's home in Washington. "How many times in the past twenty-five years I've driven past this house to show constituents the house where President Wilson spent his last years," she said. She spoke of "this age of fast and constant change," when it was "more important than ever that we preserve our rich inheritance and remember its significance—both for the present and for our future."[24]

During April she lunched with Secretary Udall, Secretary of Commerce Luther H. Hodges, and other cabinet members. When the talk turned to the interstate highway system and its impact on national parks and historic places, she noted that Udall and his department presented "a loud voice for preserving the wilderness, the National Parks, the shrines, the jewels of America."[25]

Throughout the spring, Lady Bird Johnson's public speeches touched on environmental themes. At Radcliffe she urged the young women "to improve the esthetics of our cities where 70 percent of the people now live. More than 90 percent of our population growth will occur in our metropolitan areas. If our cities are cement and asphalt jungles, the children may be wolf cubs." That same spring she told the YWCA National Convention that women "want a good home environment for our children. And, if we mean this and strive for it effectively, it encompasses a really massive attack on the part of city dwellers to demand long-range, imaginative efforts to make our cities clean, functional, and beautiful." [26]

Within the Johnson administration an environmental conscious-ness was emerging. In his Great Society speech of 22 May 1964 at the University of Michigan, the president proclaimed the need "to prevent an ugly America" because "once our natural splendor is de-stroyed, it can never be recaptured. And once man can no longer walk with beauty or wonder at nature his spirit will wither and his sustenance be wasted." [27]

To carry forward the ambitious agenda of the Great Society, the president set up individual task forces to evaluate major issues and to offer policy recommendations that could be pursued after the election. It fell to White House aide Richard Goodwin to assemble the task force on what he described as "this thing they were try-ing to put together. They weren't quite sure what it was. It was the environment, it was the quality of life, it was beauty, and it was a very amorphous and difficult subject." From Goodwin's work came a Task Force Issue Paper, "Preservation of Natural Beauty," which recommended such programs as additions to the National Parks System, laws to promote wilderness areas and wild-river systems, and the control of billboard advertising along the highways.[28]

The campaign of the Johnson administration on behalf of natural beauty and conservation was part of a general revival of the conser-vation movement that had begun in the late 1950s and had gathered momentum during the Kennedy presidency. In its beginning phase, the agenda for action centered on questions relating to "natural en-vironmental values" that involved the preservation of wilderness areas, the providing of room for recreation, and the general claims of open space against the advance of developments, roads, and construction. When Johnson became president, Udall gave him a memorandum, "The Administration and Conservation — A Look at Programs and Priorities." Udall emphasized the Land and Water

Conservation Fund, the Wilderness bill, water projects, national parks and seashores, and plans for the conversion of saltwater and the transmission of electric power. A presidential message, Udall argued, should make "an appeal to protect the quality of American life." [29]

As yet, however, there was no public environmental movement to sustain such a White House initiative, but some of the elements of such a political force were coming together by 1964. The older style of conservation, associated initially with Theodore Roosevelt and Gifford Pinchot, which stressed the efficient use of natural resources and opposed the preservation of wilderness areas, came to seem by the 1950s narrowly focused and insensitive to the threats that human pollution and a burgeoning population posed to the environment. During the postwar years, Americans saw themselves as potential users or consumers of the beauty and integrity of the land, and they worried about the quality of their lives as the natural world became degraded. Progress that might destroy the Indiana Dunes, that imperiled Storm King Mountain on the Hudson River, or that endangered the Grand Canyon had to be resisted. Those people who mounted protests against local examples of pollution and environmental decay swelled the membership lists of the Sierra Club, the Audubon Society, and garden clubs during the late 1950s and early 1960s. [30]

The publication of Rachel Carson's *Silent Spring* in 1962, which alerted a national audience to the dangers of DDT and other pesticides, was only the most celebrated event of a rising consciousness about the environment in the decade before Lyndon Johnson came to office. Young, educated, affluent citizens wanted a natural environment that would afford them access to recreational and leisure facilities as well as aesthetic experiences that would symbolize a good and harmonious society. As users of the natural bounty, they wanted to protect the environment from the threats of development, and they had the political energy to mobilize their power as voters. The foundation was present to transform the concern for "natural environmental values" of the late 1950s and early 1960s into the ecological thrust of the second half of the 1960s. [31]

John F. Kennedy supplied more vigorous presidential leadership on conservation than the nation had seen since Franklin D. Roosevelt. He sent a special message to Congress about conservation in February 1961 and followed that action with a White House Conference on conservation in May 1962. The president also encouraged Stewart Udall in his efforts in Interior and wrote a preface to the secretary's book *The Quiet Crisis* (1963). Kennedy's most significant contribution was to reassert the concept that the federal government had a primary responsibility to exercise its authority on issues of natural resources and the environment. Kennedy was instrumental in the adoption of the idea of an expanded federal role and a higher level of funding. The Johnson administration had a direct legacy from its predecessor in conservation matters, an important consideration for a new president who wished to emphasize the continuities between himself and the Kennedy years.

Lyndon Johnson did not have to be pushed to become a conservation president. In 1964 and in ensuing years, this Texas politician showed a commitment to the future of the natural heritage that enabled him to rival Theodore Roosevelt among conservationist presidents. Part of his concern came from his innate love of the land, one of the strong bonds with his wife. Originally, he admired the Texas Hill Country where he had been raised, and once he took office he embraced the broader national landscape. "I have a lot of land," he told his Task Force on Natural Beauty in July 1964, "and I only wish that all the people could have the chance to experience the same joys that I can. I am concerned with the erosion of natural beauty in this country; I know that this is a problem which cuts across many lines."[32] Beyond this aspect of his conservation spirit, Lyndon Johnson saw himself as carrying forward Franklin Roosevelt's tradition of support for natural resources and extending the Kennedy legacy. The program also coincided with the goals of the Great Society, which spoke about the overall quality of national life.

Behind the scenes, Lady Bird Johnson was an important agent for the Natural Beauty initiative in 1964. Stewart Udall believed that "she influenced the president to demand—and support—more farsighted conservation legislation"; he was also convinced that "Ladybird's pushing" increased her husband's receptivity to conservation initiatives. To avoid claiming credit for herself about legislation or ideas that were properly those of Lyndon Johnson, his wife, after leaving the White House, rarely made direct connections about her influence on specific conservation decisions. However, as her expertise about the subject demonstrated, she had a significant impact on the president's thinking in this area.[33]

During summer 1964 Lyndon Johnson created a Task Force on Natural Beauty, with Prof. Charles M. Haar of Harvard University as its chair. The eleven-member task force, which included Laurance S. Rockefeller, John Kenneth Galbraith, Jane Jacobs, and Loren Eisley, met with the president on 31 July. Johnson wanted them "to paint me a picture . . . of how we can preserve a beautiful America." They should not worry about how their recommendations might fare in Congress. The president would consider their ideas and send to Capitol Hill "what I think is fitting." After the president left, the group defined its areas of responsibility. Their goal, Haar said later, was "to capture the conscience of the king." The task force did not yet know, he recalled, "of the great interest of Mrs. Johnson in this operation, nor that the president was going to make this one of his very carefully nurtured babies." But by midsummer the Task Force on Natural Beauty was assembling the elements of a new conservation impetus for the Johnson administration.[34]

At almost the same time, Mrs. Johnson made a trip through the Rocky Mountain West to visit Indian reservations and national parks in the region. The trip was also designed to help the reelection prospects of Senators Gale McGee of Wyoming and Frank Moss of Utah, both running in an area where Barry M. Goldwater seemed strong. The tour not only helped them win their races, but it also gave the First Lady time to discuss conservation issues with Secretary Udall, who accompanied her through this country that he knew so well. As they sat together on the propellor-driven plane, they talked about the landscape that lay below them. Another working partnership was being formed.

Stewart Lee Udall was forty-four years old that summer. Born in St. Johns, Arizona, to Mormon parents, he had attended the University of Arizona and served as an air gunner in Europe during World War II. After college and law school, he ran for Congress in 1954 and served three terms. His ability to deliver the Arizona delegation for Kennedy led to a place in the cabinet. Udall's quick movements evoked memories for many people of his years as a guard on the Arizona basketball team.

Udall brought energy and commitment to conservation and to the Interior Department, but it took him some years to become an effective administrator. In his spare moments, usually on long plane trips, he wrote *The Quiet Crisis,* which made him a national conservation figure. "America today stands poised on a pinnacle of wealth and power," he wrote in the book's foreword, "yet we live in a land of vanishing beauty, of increasing ugliness, of shrinking open space, and of an overall environment that is diminished daily by pollution and noise and blight." [35]

Udall had not expected to remain in the Johnson cabinet because he had thwarted the Texan's bid to secure Arizona's seventeen delegates in 1960. The president's "long memory" would most likely remove him from the job he loved. But Lyndon Johnson saw Udall as another symbol of continuity with the Kennedys. More important, the two men shared a feeling for the land of the Southwest. The bond drew them together in a way that Udall had not experienced with Jack Kennedy, a man of the sea and the shore. [36]

Udall emerged as a significant voice for the environment in the Johnson administration. He later recalled that under both the presidents he served, he "had pretty much of a free hand." Although he was glad that "there was very little that was initiated at the White House in my area," Udall also kept himself in presidential favor by his support of the First Lady's urban-beautification efforts and his endorsement of billboard control. Like President Johnson himself, Udall was in transition from the older style of conservation to the newer rhythms of environmentalism. His partnership with the Johnsons was strong and productive until it frayed at the end of the administration. [37]

In April 1964, Liz Carpenter suggested that Lady Bird Johnson make a western trip to see Indian reservations and national parks, and Udall took up the idea with enthusiasm. "No First Lady within memory has gone to an Indian reservation to make a survey of conditions," he noted. The trip was scheduled for 14–17 August, with ceremonies that included dedicating a dam, making a speech at the University of Utah, and political appearances, in addition to the visits to the reservations. [38]

When she spoke on the trip, Lady Bird Johnson talked about the quality of the landscape. "The interesting thing about Park City," she told residents of that Utah community, "is that you have developed the one resource that is least exhaustible, your natural beauty." At the University of Utah on 15 August, she asserted, "This American society can never achieve [the] destiny it seeks, can never remove the slums or the prejudice, or the ugliness, unless citizens join in the great adventure of our time." At the dedication of Flaming Gorge Dam, she told the audience, "Enjoy the beauty of your hills and protect it for your children." Udall called the trip a political tour de force. "Mrs. Johnson was extremely effective on her 'land and people' tour in the West last week," he reported to the president. "Her interest in the out-of-doors and her concern for conservation have a national impact that is the finest kind of presidential politics."[39]

The conversations between Udall and the First Lady on the western swing laid the basis for their productive working relationship. They found, Udall said, an "instant rapport" on conservation issues, and Mrs. Johnson displayed "an instinctive feeling for the beauty of the country." From her countless questions, Udall became convinced that she had decided to make "a major commitment of her time" to the environment and beautification. The trip also underlined that the First Lady could be a potent campaigner. "I think she came back with considerable confidence" Udall declared.[40]

A week after the trip, on 24 August, the Democratic National Convention opened in Atlantic City, New Jersey. As Lyndon Johnson prepared to go to the convention, he was still saying to his wife "the same old refrain" that "he did not believe he should accept the nomination." Lady Bird Johnson knew that the president regularly acted this way before plunging into a campaign. Still, she had "reason to think he didn't want to run previous to 1964," and "he was wrestling with that demon very hard." As early as mid-June he had showed her a statement removing himself from the race. After long talks with him on 25 August and much walking, she wrote to Lyndon: "To step out now would be wrong for your country, and I can see nothing but a lonely wasteland for your future. Your friends would be frozen in an embarrassed silence and your enemies jeering." She later recalled in her diary, "I do not remember hours I ever found harder." Although the extent to which Johnson was ever serious about withdrawal is questionable, his wife's letter provided him some degree of reassurance, once it had been, in her words, "put in front of him, sort of inescapable." [41]

In the campaign that followed Johnson's nomination, the high point for Lady Bird Johnson came in early October, when the Lady Bird Special made a whistle-stop tour through the heart of the South. The Civil Rights Act of 1964 and the racial liberalism of the Johnson administration had loosened Democratic ties in Dixie. Passions for Barry Goldwater ran high. After a two-week drive along the Gulf Coast, a southern woman reported that "she never saw anything but Goldwater bumper stickers any place on the trip." [42]

Faced with this surge of Republican sentiment among southern whites, the Johnsons did not intend to let their native region slip into the Republican column without a fight. Their own experience and the rising force of the civil rights movement had led both of them away from the prejudices of their region. Mrs. Johnson recalled that her native East Texas "was heavily populated by blacks, and it was the hardest place in Texas for civil rights changes to be made." As a child she had heard of an episode in which a band of white man had first "cornered a black man in the middle of the night and accused him of some crime." When the man tried to escape, "the white men shot him in the back." She recalled thinking to herself, "This isn't right. Somebody ought to change this." [43]

The frequent automobile rides from Washington to Texas with their black household employees had further shown Lady Bird Johnson the human burden of segregation. In Memphis, on one trip, Mrs. Johnson asked a female motel operator whether her maid Zephyr Wright and another African-American woman who was traveling with them might stay overnight. "No," responded the woman; "we work 'em but we don't sleep 'em." Mrs. Johnson replied, "That's a nasty way to be," and drove on. Still, the First Lady believed that the South should not be written off in the Democratic canvass. "We must go," she said; "we must let them know that we love the South." She convinced the president, against his initial political instincts, to let her make the trip. For Lady Bird Johnson, it was to be "a journey of the heart." [44]

She approached the campaign with her usual care and thoroughness. "Don't give me the easy towns, Liz," she told Carpenter; "anyone can get into Atlanta—it's the new modern South. Let me take the tough ones." Relying on the Democratic National Committee, the White House, and seventy men and women who were doing advance work in the South, Carpenter and the First Lady mapped out a 1,700-mile trip through Virginia, the Carolinas, Florida, Georgia, Alabama, Mississippi, and Louisiana. Mrs. Johnson said to the advance staff, "I feel at home in the small towns, and I want my speeches to make the people feel I am at home too." She was ready to defend the president's policies because "I know the Civil Rights Act was right and I don't mind saying so. But I'm tired of people making the South the whipping boy of the Democratic party." Before the trip had been publicly announced, she called the governors and senators of the states she would visit to invite them on board the train and to ask for their support. Senator Willis Robertson of Virginia had planned "antelope hunting," and another politician was still mourning his wife, who had died two years earlier. Mrs. Johnson's calls induced five governors to join her, however, and four senators signed on as well.[45]

The trip grew in size and interest as 6 October neared. No First Lady had gone out on this kind of personal campaign swing for her husband before, and the press found the tour an entertaining novelty in what otherwise seemed a Johnson walkover. Three hundred people, including a press contingent of over 200, left on the nineteen cars of the Lady Bird Special from Union Station around 7:00 A.M. on 6 October. The car from which Mrs. Johnson would speak had been painted red, white, and blue, provided with an awning, and decorated with flowers by Bess Abell and her staff. The president made the first stop in Alexandria, Virginia, and joined them again later, once in North Carolina and at the end in New Orleans. After he had left the first time, the train was off on a rollicking and exciting old-time stump swing. Reporters munched LBJ's pickled okra, enjoyed the daily happy hour, and read Liz Carpenter's "Dixie Dictionary," which defined "kissin' kin" as "anyone who will come to the depot." [46]

At each stop, Lady Bird Johnson included deft local touches into her prepared remarks. "The law to assure equal rights passed by Congress last July with three-fourths of the Republicans joining two-thirds of the Democrats has been received by the South for the most part in a way that is a great credit to local leadership," she said in Alexandria, Virginia; and she stressed economic prosperity as a more important asset to the region than clinging to racial prejudices. In Virginia and North Carolina, she noted, per capita income was up over that of 1960, and "I would be remiss if I did not point out that these were Democratic years." As the audiences responded to her, she exclaimed to Liz Carpenter, "I love it. I'm like Br'er Rabbit in the briar patch." Congressman Hale Boggs of Louisiana, warming up the crowds, shouted that the Johnsons were as "much a part of the South as tobacco and cotton and peanuts and grits and redeye gravy." Southern politicians suddenly found that being seen on the train had become the thing to do.[47]

Not every stop was a love fest. In the Carolinas, hecklers waved posters reading, "Lady Bird, Lady Bird, fly away"; and in Charleston signs on the homes announced, "This house is sold on Goldwater." Male politicians on the train wanted to strike back when interruptions and jeering occurred during Mrs. Johnson's speeches. She declined, saying, "I know you're chivalrous and they make you mad, but I didn't expect this to be an easy assignment. I'll handle it." She stopped her speech, looked at the hecklers, and said, "I respect your right to think as you do. Now I'm asking you to be quiet while I finish what I have to say." Usually that request brought silence, and Republican leaders asked publicly that the taunting stop.[48]

After four days of towns, speeches, grimy reporters, and a festive atmosphere, the Lady Bird Special ended its run in New Orleans. President Johnson joined his wife and made a major speech on civil rights that night. The First Lady's campaigning had been a decided success. "Not since the days of Franklin Roosevelt have so many Southern Democratic leaders openly thrown their lot in with the national ticket," wrote one reporter. Nevertheless, the trip did not reverse Goldwater's inroads or Republican sentiment in the South. Four states in which she had campaigned went Republican in the fall election. Her appearances did, however, underscore Democratic interest in the South and may have minimized defections from the party. For Mrs. Johnson herself, the Lady Bird Special was a sign of her clear emergence as a public figure on her own terms. She had set a precedent for First Ladies in her personal campaigning, and she had brought it off in style. The organizational skills that Carpenter, Abell, and Lady Bird Johnson's staff had shown would carry over

Lady Bird Special Menu, October 1964. (author's collection)

into the beautification work ahead. The trip had been, Mrs. Johnson wrote later, "those four most dramatic days in my political life." [49]

She displayed another side of her character a few days after the trip ended. Presidential assistant Walter W. Jenkins had been arrested at the Washington YMCA and had been charged with having had homosexual relations with a sixty-year-old man on 7 October. A week later the incident came to light, along with a previous episode in 1959. While the president said nothing publicly, the First

Lady immediately issued a statement: "My heart is aching today for someone who has reached the end point of exhaustion in dedicated service to his country." President Johnson released his own statement later that same day, and the incident rapidly faded from public attention. By her independent action, his wife had done what was right under the circumstances and also had prevented a minor flap from becoming a greater embarrassment.[50]

During the last three weeks of the campaign, Lady Bird Johnson stumped through the Southwest with the wives of three cabinet members and made other stops in Pennsylvania, Kentucky, and Indiana on her own. In the final days she joined the president in crisscrossing the West and the Midwest before the voting on 3 November. They celebrated the landslide victory over Goldwater at the Municipal Auditorium in Austin, and then they returned to the LBJ Ranch for ten days, to rest from the campaign and to plan for the term ahead. "My chief emotions," Mrs. Johnson wrote later, "were simply satisfaction in people's faith in Lyndon and a renewed determination to help him use the next four years to the best of his ability and to make some steps forward."[51]

Her own first year in the White House had been a time of beginnings and testing. She and her staff had learned about the demands of organizing trips, having speeches prepared, and accommodating the needs of the press. Lady Bird Johnson had overcome her earlier fears of public speaking and had succeeded, in the Lady Bird Special, in establishing herself as a skilled campaigner. It remained for her to identify issues and subjects that she could pursue during a full presidential term. To that question she turned within a few days of the election and soon concluded that natural beauty, or "beautification" had the capacity to "make my heart sing." Beginning in Washington, DC, she launched a movement that became an important element in the heightened conservation spirit of the 1960s and that helped to expand the horizons of the institution of the First Lady.[52]

CHAPTER 3

WAYS TO BEAUTIFY AMERICA

During the weeks after the 1964 presidential election victory, Lady Bird Johnson received suggestions from a number of her friends and advisers about what she should do as First Lady in the four years that lay ahead. One project to which she devoted much attention was the Head Start program for preschool children. She was "present at its birth in the Red Room when a small group of believers in it—some social workers, Sargent Shriver and I—met to explore and discuss whether or not the program would work." Once the Head Start initiative had been launched, she threw her prestige behind it. On 19 February 1965 she enlisted a number of governors' wives and celebrities to come to the White House. Their goal was to see that "no child shall be doomed to be a drop-out from school, or in a larger sense, from our economic and cultural life."[1]

The publicity that surrounded the meeting stimulated intense popular interest in the new program. As director of the Office of Economic Opportunity, Sargent Shriver reported that his office had received 2,000 postcards from the public: "Headstart, in short, seems to be zooming to the heights." He planned to increase the number of children involved from the original target of 100,000 to somewhere between 300,000 and 500,000 in 1965.[2]

In the months that followed her initial commitment, Lady Bird Johnson lent her name and support to a wide range of public activi-

ties designed to promote awareness of Head Start. She arranged theatrical programs and wrote introductions for articles about nutri-
tion and other needs of preschoolers. In mid-August she visited the
Head Start program in New Jersey and spent a busy day visiting centers and seeing the children. "You have to start somewhere to break
the cycle," she wrote in her diary, "and this is the time, the malleable
age." So successful was Head Start in its early stages that the demand
for its services soon exceeded the available money. In December
1965, Shriver assured her that Head Start would reach up to 1 million
children in the year ahead.[3]

As funding for the Great Society encountered problems in Congress with the escalation of the Vietnam War, appropriations for
Head Start lagged. The First Lady received recurrent complaints
about the need for more money and more centers. In June 1966 she
and Shriver exchanged letters attesting to the value of Head Start
and its tangible results. "The report on the progress of Head Start,"
Mrs. Johnson wrote, "and the many accomplishments [are] most rewarding to all who have put their hearts and efforts into the project."
The episode revealed the extent to which Mrs. Johnson used her
prestige to encourage the continuance of a viable social program.
During the remaining two years of the Johnson presidency, she
lobbied to keep Head Start in existence and to broaden its coverage
of needy children. In April 1968 Shriver told her, "You provided the
most crucial help to Head Start" and to other Office of Economic
Opportunity programs.[4]

Although Lady Bird Johnson's work for Head Start was invalu-
able, it did not become her first priority for the Johnson presidency.
During the final weeks of 1964, when she was debating what to emphasize, she decided that "the whole field of conservation and beautification" had "the greatest appeal." In large and small ways, she
began to implement the initiative that became associated with her
years in Washington.[5]

Within a few days of the election, she induced the president to call
Secretary of Commerce Luther Hodges about junkyards along the
highways, and she launched what in time became the effort to enact
highway-beautification legislation. At the same time, she asked close
friends and policymakers to provide her with ideas about how a
campaign to improve the look of the United States might proceed.
Secretary of the Interior Stewart Udall weighed in first with the

recommendation that Mrs. Johnson transform Washington, DC into " 'a garden city' whose floral displays and plantings would make it a handsome model for America." Udall was on "cloud nine" when he received the invitation to come to Texas, and he became even happier as they discussed how to begin with Washington so as to set an example for the rest of the nation. Udall set about developing ways in which the Interior Department could carry forward and participate in the First Lady's initiative.[6]

Parallel to Udall's effort were similar suggestions from Washington friends such as Elizabeth "Libby" Rowe that "you extend your interest in the White House's beauty and history to the entire city." The wife of James Rowe, a sometime political adviser to Lyndon Johnson and influential Democratic lawyer, Libby Rowe was a native Washingtonian and the chair of the National Capital Planning Commission. She proposed that a "White House Committee on Washington's appearance" be established, and she suggested names of city officials and public-spirited citizens as potential members. Rowe's letter was an important milestone in the early stages of beautification planning in Washington.[7]

As a shrewd political operator, Lady Bird Johnson rarely limited herself to one set of advisers or to a single line of action. She enlisted Katherine "Katie" Louchheim, an assistant deputy secretary in the State Department and a major figure among Democratic women, and Antonia Chayes — a lawyer in the Kennedy White House and a consultant at the National Institute of Mental Health — to provide their own ideas about the city's appearance. She also drew in Mary Lasker, a New York philanthropist, an advocate of urban beauty, and a diligent lobbyist for health legislation as another possible source of beautification concepts to consider.

Ideas came in quickly. The proposals focused generally on using Washington, DC as an example of how beautification could enhance the quality of life for all Americans in a manner befitting the Great Society. Chayes contended, for example, that cities "should offer people the chance to grow and live a full life" and therefore that playgrounds and parks belonged not only in the "good neighborhoods" but everywhere. "These are goals that go beyond survival — beyond breaking the circle of poverty. These goals reach for the 'Great Society.' "[8]

On 11 December, Lady Bird Johnson talked with Katie Louchheim

Lady Bird Johnson and Mary Lasker, 5 February 1965.
(LBJ Library photograph, 33841-1)

at the White House about a "possible beautification campaign" for
Washington. Her commitment was cautious at this point, but it expanded soon. In a luncheon meeting with Rowe and Louchheim
four days later it was decided that she would encourage private and
governmental efforts toward beautification and preservation. "Mrs.
Johnson's sponsorship would inspire wide support of both a private and governmental nature and generally interest the nation in
this beautification and preservation process precisely as Mrs. Kennedy had done with the historic renovation of the White House."
Her initial emphasis would be on Washington, with its parks, Mall,
and historical landmarks, "and the beautification of all new urban
renewal projects and public housing units." [9]

The decision to focus first on Washington, DC was logical because the nation's capital had already come under criticism for its
deteriorating condition and mounting social problems. It was also

solely under the control of the federal government, and there would be no institutional barriers to what the First Lady wished to attempt. "Washington is a shabby city," Udall told the First Lady, and outside critics made the same point. There was the "official Washington" of monuments, parks, and public buildings, and the "other Washington," where most of the city's residents lived in ghettos and run-down neighborhoods. Both Washingtons faced significant problems when the Johnson administration took power. Pollution, highway location and construction, inadequate transportation, and a decaying inner city—these issues made Washington a case study of the urban problems that the nation faced in the 1960s. To the mix was added the city's subordinate relationship to Congress, which ran it "like some territorial possession." Even more crucial was the black majority in Washington, impoverished and segregated, with a white minority in economic and political control. The black residents of Washington, one writer observed, were "on a sidetrack of the American way of life." [10]

John Kennedy had wanted to make Washington "to a degree, a showcase for our culture." He tried to enhance respect for the city's older buildings and to upgrade the quality of federal edifices. He started an initiative to improve the appearance of Pennsylvania Avenue. The president's wry remark that "Washington has the charm of a Northern city and the efficiency of a Southern one" caught the spirit of his concern for the capital's affairs. The president even named a special assistant for District of Columbia policy as evidence of his interest in the city's fate. Nonetheless, in the mid-1960s, Washington was still very much "a lost colony—still surviving—barely—on the American continent." [11]

By December 1964, Mrs. Johnson had several personal campaigns under way to promote beautification. Improvement of the look of the nation's highways had begun, and negotiations over the control of junkyards and billboards were in motion, an issue that would run parallel to her other work on natural beauty in 1965. Invitations were being readied for the First Lady's Committee. She also knew that the president would refer to natural beauty in his State of the Union address on 4 January 1965. [12]

Lady Bird Johnson was moving into uncharted areas for a First Lady in shaping the beautification campaign during late 1964. Other

presidential wives had pursued enactment of a single piece of legislation (Ellen Wilson and Jacqueline Kennedy) or had been identified
with broad social themes (Eleanor Roosevelt and world peace). But
there had not been a previous example of a sustained programmatic
initiative with which a First Lady had been identified. In that sense,
the projected natural beauty campaign illustrated how much of an
innovator Lady Bird Johnson wanted to be in the White House.

In his remarks to Congress, Lyndon Johnson said that "for over
three centuries the beauty of America has sustained our spirit and
enlarged our vision." The nation had to act "to protect this heritage." Giving the first State of the Union speech to mention natural
beauty, Johnson called for more parks, landscaping of highways,
and the power for government to act on pollution. He said that he
would summon a White House Conference on Natural Beauty in the
spring. Mrs. Johnson observed after the speech, "I have lived with it
and helped hammer it out." She wrote in her diary, "I hope we can
do something about that in our four years here." [13]

During the following month, Lady Bird Johnson organized her
committee. She sent out invitations asking prospective members to
attend a meeting at the White House on 11 February 1965 to "stimu-
late new interest in making our city truly beautiful for the people
who live here and come here." One important ally was the philanthropist and conservation advocate, Laurance Rockefeller. She met
with him and his wife on 3 February to talk about the projected
White House Conference on Natural Beauty. "Getting on the subject
of beautification is like picking up a tangle skein of wool—all the
threads are interwoven," she wrote in her diary entry for that day;
"recreation and pollution and mental health, and the crime rate, and
rapid transit, and highway beautification, and the war on poverty,
and parks—national, state, and local." As she thought about Rockefeller and the conference, she added, "There are many of us desper-
ately interested in something positive coming out of this program,
something besides a lot of words and proliferation of committees." [14]

President Johnson added to the interest in the environment with
his separate 8 February message on natural beauty: "A growing
population is swallowing up areas of natural beauty with its demands for living space, and is placing increased demand on our
overburdened areas of recreation and pleasure." He called for a "new

conservation" that would emphasize "restoration and innovation." Among the programs he advocated were highway beautification, clean-air legislation, and the White House Conference on Natural Beauty, which was to meet in May. By legitimizing natural beauty in the first presidential message devoted to the subject, Johnson advanced his own environmental agenda and gave a powerful impetus to his wife's work in the same area.[15]

Three days later, the First Lady's Committee assembled in the Blue Room of the White House. Its organizing members included Elizabeth Rowe, Katie Louchheim, and Mary Lasker, along with such important local and national figures as Laurance Rockefeller, Walter Washington of the District, and the architect Nathaniel Owings. Mrs. Johnson said that her committee should have as its goal "to implement what is already under way, supplement what should be under way, and to be the catalyst for action." Mrs. Johnson led the committee into a discussion of programs for the city that included planting flowers in the traffic triangles and squares, awards for neighborhood beautification projects, and revitalization of monumental areas. Subcommittees were named and went to work on specific projects.[16]

The First Lady promoted her initiative with a widely read interview in *U.S. News and World Report,* "Ways to Beautify America," late in February. She told the reporters that "ugliness is so grim. A little beauty, something that is lovely, I think, can help create harmony which will lessen tensions." She was cautious about billboard control because "it's a big industry," but she predicted that "public feeling is going to bring about regulation, so that you don't have a solid diet of billboards on all the roads." She took the reporters through the whole range of environmental topics, and then argued, "The time is ripe — the time is now — to take advantage of this yeasty, bubbling desire to beautify our cities and our countryside. I hope all Americans will join in this effort."[17]

Enthusiastic citizens responded to her call for improving the look of the nation. Phone messages poured into the White House from Washingtonians first and then from across America. "Bravo Mr. President," said the Women's Chamber of Commerce of Atlanta. A reporter noted that "natural beauty is a political natural," citing the remark of "a presidential supporter" that "there's intellectual

The gracious hostess. (Center for American History, University of Texas at Austin, Ferguson [Henry Noel] photograph, CN08211)

interest in all of this and there's interest from the four-buck-an-hour factory worker who has an outboard in the garage." The journalist James Perry also noted that Mrs. Johnson's "rebellion against ugliness" seemed "as genuine and deep-seated as the president's, and surely she is as influential with her husband as any First Lady we've seen in this century." [18]

At this time, however, few observers looked into the historical roots of the natural beauty initiative. There began to be some reservations expressed about the term beautification itself and whether it represented the best statement of what the president and First Lady were trying to accomplish. Were the goals of Mrs. Johnson and her committee essentially cosmetic, and did they leave the real problems of the cities and the landscape unaddressed? The journalist Wolf Von Eckardt expressed this view when he said beautification would leave "our real problems" unsolved if nothing more occurred than "sprinkling wildflower seeds along highways, getting rid of automobile junkyards, billboards, overhead wiring, smog and water pollution alone—important as all this is."[19]

Lady Bird Johnson, without knowing it, had touched on the troubled historical legacy of the City Beautiful movement that dated from the beginning of the twentieth century. That impulse had two parts. In the area of large city planning, Chicago, Washington, and other large urban centers sought to combine aesthetics in the design of the metropolis. Parks, railroad stations, public buildings, and broad avenues were created that fused "naturalistic park systems with classicistic civic centers."[20] Running parallel with this concern to beautify the monumental parts of the nation's larger cities was a socially based, citizen-driven effort to improve and upgrade the appearance of smaller cities and localities. Women were strongly represented in the 2,400 or so civic-improvement groups that sprang up during the Progressive Era. The purpose behind these campaigns was not just to improve for the sake of improvement; these reformers wanted "to make our America a better and more beautiful place to live in." The City Beautiful campaigns at the beginning of the twentieth century were an aspect of the optimistic reformism of the Progressive Era.[21]

The concepts of the clean and efficient city, both large and small, arose at the same time and often enlisted the same people in its campaigns. Junior Sanitation Leagues and Junior Health Leagues, largely sponsored by concerned women, carried on city-cleanup days and antilitter campaigns. They spoke of Municipal Housekeeping and conducted Clean Up and Paint Up drives in 5,000 places in 1915. A woman in Binghamton, New York, used language that foreshadowed what Lady Bird Johnson would say half a century later: "We must picture to our children . . . how each one of us has pride in his home, and wants it to be as perfect as possible, and how that feeling extends to its surroundings, to the lawns and streets in the vicinity. Then in a broader way we think of the city as our home."[22]

Despite the accomplishments of the City Beautiful movement in

the first two decades of the century, it came under fire from architects and city planners for its alleged superficiality in dealing with
the city's problems at the time of World War I. The City Beautiful
was too simple an idea, said the rising breed of city planners, to deal
with the hard issues of zoning, sanitation, and housing. Beautification seemed less and less relevant and important. In time even the
term beautification came to have a negative edge. It carried a feminine tinge because of the role of garden clubs and roadside councils
in pursuing improvement of roads and parks. The male-dominated
world of architecture reacted with skepticism to any program that
might bring women into their preserve. When Lady Bird Johnson
embarked on beautification, she understood the problem that she
faced, even if she did not know the historical background of her dilemma. Beautification, she said "sounds cosmetic and trivial and it's
prissy." She did not realize that there had been an active tradition
of women's involvement in beautification earlier in the century to
which she might have appealed to support her own initiative.[23]

The problem of what to call her campaign would plague the First
Lady for the rest of her time in the White House and beyond. As
her aide Sharon Francis said, "We all, I believe, suffered from the
wrong word, and Mrs. Johnson asked us to use the word beautification as little as possible." Liz Carpenter made the same point: "It
just seemed to rise up, and it was never a word we were totally satisfied with, but the alternatives were stodgy and they didn't sound
like anything new. Conservation. Environmental beauty. Nothing."
The heart of the difficulty was that Lady Bird Johnson and those
around her shared the view, well expressed by a member of the Task
Force for Natural Beauty, that beautification "sort of has a feminine
aura to it, you know, and it's something sissy-like." When Lyndon
Johnson talked about beauty, in contrast, "it became a much more
masculine approach, and it became much more talking of natural
parks and society. It became much more acceptable."[24]

As a woman of her time and her region, Lady Bird Johnson accepted the idea that the feminine implications of beautification had
to be muted and restrained. Unaware of the tradition of women in
conservation and not yet a feminist herself, she concurred in the implicit inferiority of women that the word beautification evoked. She
and her colleagues sometimes spoke condescendingly themselves of

"garden club ladies" or invoked the stereotypes of "old ladies in ten-
nis shoes or puttering gentlemen in tweeds with a rose cutting in
their hands." Social disdain for any taint of homosexuality was not
far below the surface of such remarks.[25]

Given the political role she had chosen as First Lady, her husband's sexist attitudes, and the real constraints of a chauvinistic
Washington and nation, her attitude toward beautification as a word
made sense in the short run. There were lasting negative conse-
quences, too. Since beauty was such an ill-defined and easily mocked
concept, her program could be showered with masculine sarcasm
whenever opponents wished to make cheap points. Her male supporters could respond only in a tentative and an uneasy manner,
lest they seem unmanly in their views. There was always an un-
deserved tone of apology and supplication about what Lady Bird
Johnson did for the environment; it arose from the label beautification. In its way, her campaign became an instructive lesson in how
constricted the role was that women, even a First Lady, played in
American public life in the 1960s.

Despite her initial lack of sophistication about the range of issues
that beautification could touch, Lady Bird Johnson operated from
environmental premises as sound as those of her critics. The First
Lady never believed that simple cleanups would be enough. In 1965
she told a financial columnist that she wanted to move "from the
garden club to the hardware stage of the problem," and she sought
to address the impact of business on the landscape as much as she
could. Moreover, her emphasis on the environmental problems of
the cities represented an important shift from the rural focus of
the early twentieth century. She wanted to involve as many citizens as possible in beautification, and she rejected few remedies and
left few options unexplored. She also believed that a work accomplished was better than an incompleted vision. Thus her campaign,
even in its initial stages, looked back to the citizen idealism that had
first sparked the City Beautiful movement while it simultaneously
tapped the local consciousness about environmental deterioration
that spurred the ecological movement during the next decade.[26]

In 1965, popular interest in the First Lady's appeal for beautification produced an upsurge in her mail at the White House. As a result, her staff expanded with the addition of two aides who became

key participants in her environmental work. Sharon Francis came first. A native of the Pacific Northwest and a graduate of Mount Holyoke College, she had worked for the Wilderness Society before joining Udall's staff in the Interior Department. She met Lady Bird Johnson in December 1964 during a White House meeting. When the First Lady entered the room on that cold, snowy afternoon, the singing of civil rights marchers outside the fence was audible. Mrs. Johnson asked, "What are they doing?" and Francis responded, "They're singing 'We Shall Overcome,' and they're kneeling in the snow, Mrs. Johnson." As Francis turned to look at the First Lady, she saw "a tear coming down the side of her face."[27]

Francis joined the First Lady's staff in March to help with the growing flow of beautification mail, and she soon acquired a full-time position. Eventually she obtained her own office, and by September she was officially a "staff assistant for beautification." Assistants assigned to push specific programs were a new development for a First Lady and reflected how Lady Bird Johnson was stretching the institution to accommodate her own goals and priorities. Dubbed the East Wing Egghead by Liz Carpenter, Francis became a combination of speechwriter, a link with conservation groups, and a source of environmental ideas for her boss.[28]

Joining Sharon Francis was Cynthia Wilson. A journalism degree from the University of Texas was Wilson's ticket into the White House, and she came on board in early 1965. Wilson was devoted to conservation causes, and she functioned as an all-purpose "inside" implementer for the First Lady. She wrote press releases, did advance work on trips, and monitored the incoming correspondence for information about controversies and possible problems. Wilson and Francis created a solid working combination, and Lady Bird Johnson's staff operated smoothly throughout her White House years.[29]

As the new campaign got under way, Mrs. Johnson looked for new approaches and fresh ideas to provide to her committee. At the panel's second meeting, they heard architect Nathaniel Owings present his ideas for improving Washington's Mall. The members then boarded minibuses for a trip to the Mall and "our first planting." Later, at the triangle between Maryland and Independence Avenues, at Third Street, SW, the First Lady put in the first azaleas. At the urging of Walter Washington, the "entourage of committee and press" went to Greenleaf Gardens, a black housing area. Two school bands serenaded the minibuses, and then Mrs. Johnson spoke briefly. Afterward she told Stewart Udall "that all of our efforts will fail unless these people in these neighborhoods can see the challenge and do the work in their own front yards." [30]

Behind the public face of the committee there were disagreements about the direction the campaign should take. Aides to Udall worried that assigning Walter Washington to black neighborhood issues while the representatives of the Garden Clubs went to well-to-do neighborhoods might send the wrong impression about the First Lady's goals. Others fretted about the perennial issue of superficiality and whether the White House was sufficiently aware of the matter.

Lady Bird Johnson had already begun to address these questions. She met for two hours on 17 March with Secretary and Mrs. Udall, Elizabeth Rowe, Sharon Francis, and Nash Castro of the National Park Service to explore what beautification "could mean for the United States in five or ten years." The First Lady told them that her mail revealed that the American people were "ready for higher aesthetic standards" and that the committee could be a means to "express these thoughts." She wanted to act as an inspirational and encouraging force to persuade citizens to beautify their own surroundings. Cleanup programs and projects, such as the ones that Walter Washington had advocated, improved the physical environment and resulted "in an increased sense of neighborliness and community pride among the participants." Responding to the popular upsurge of interest in beautification, Lady Bird Johnson was already moving beyond the limited role that she had set for herself in December 1964.[31]

By the time the committee held its third meeting on 8 April 1965, its work had become more institutionalized. Udall provided a stenographer who made a transcript of the session, and that practice continued as long as the committee operated. There was an abundance of news. Mary Lasker had donated more than 9,000 azaleas to upgrade Pennsylvania Avenue. From the Japanese government came 4,000 cherry trees, though in the end the trees had to be American plants grown from Japanese roots because the native Japanese trees carried a dangerous virus. The largest single gift was $100,000 from

Laurance Rockefeller, some of which was to be allocated to the improvement of the Watts Branch area, consisting of thirty-six acres in a low-income part of Northeast Washington; the rest was to be used in cleaning green oxide from statues in the city.

In her comments to the panel, Mrs. Johnson noted that the demand for speakers on beautification had grown to a point that Lee Udall, Stewart's wife, had arranged a speakers' bureau composed of Senate and cabinet wives to fill the out-of-town requests that Mrs. Johnson could not meet. Sharon Francis and Liz Carpenter had assembled kits of background materials for the speakers to use, and in spring 1965 an abundance of opportunities opened for these volunteers to spread the First Lady's message. The use of surrogates for the president's wife to act as an informal publicity apparatus was another innovation that Lady Bird Johnson developed.

Mrs. Johnson's campaign received an additional boost in April when the *Reader's Digest* reprinted in its May issue the *U.S. News and World Report*'s interview. The magazine wanted to make a formal presentation of the issue to Mrs. Johnson, a move that the White House forestalled, lest she become too associated with an individual commercial enterprise. Instead, the Let's Beautify America forum and workshop was held in Washington on 28 April, with eleven local and national beautification figures exchanging ideas about strategies for improving the nation's appearance. On that same day the First Lady held a Women Doers luncheon on neighborhood beautification.

The following month Mrs. Johnson made the first tour devoted explicitly to beautification in what became a pattern during the rest of her years in Washington. She believed that it was necessary to bring her ideas and her presence to areas of the nation known for scenic beauty or where environmental problems existed. Also she knew that she needed, as Liz Carpenter put it, "to escape from behind that big iron fence around the White House once in awhile and get the feel of the country." For her it was good "to get out in the open and come to terms with things."[32]

The first region selected was closeby, the historic sites in Virginia that constituted Landscapes and Landmarks. On 11 May she set out with the Udalls, the Rockefellers, Mrs. Hubert Humphrey, several cabinet wives, and assorted highway and beautification experts.

Behind the First Lady's party came a press bus, with some forty reporters and crews from the major television networks. As the bus rolled along, Mrs. Johnson compared the view from Interstate 95 with what she had seen as they moved down Highway 1. The interstate, "a beautiful drive," was "a model of what can be done, and the median strip is a great plus." Highway 1 offered a less attractive picture. "A narrow right-of-way with uncontrolled access," the state road impressed her as "a tunnel of filling stations, billboards, neon signs, and dilapidated little buildings." She concluded that "the contrast of frenetic billboards on one road and only nature on the other was a significant lesson." [33]

The trip proved that beautification outings offered a deft way to publicize the campaign in settings that attracted press coverage and national attention. Mrs. Johnson realized that the celebrity aspects of her position presented her with the opportunity to transform popular fascination with the activities of the First Lady into an asset for her larger objectives in beautification. She became increasingly adroit in offering to the media moments when the positive qualities of her beautification work might be seen in newsworthy settings.

With the approach of the White House Conference on Natural Beauty, the pace of events related to the gathering intensified. The ABC–TV network had begun preparations for a special on Washington, DC and the First Lady for airing in the fall. She hoped that it would "speak to the whole country and sow some seeds of interest in nationwide beautification." The Johnsons were also starting a quiet campaign to persuade the philanthropist Joseph Hirshhorn to donate his collection of modern art to the Smithsonian Institution. After wooing the prospective donor, she observed in her diary, "What a situation I find myself in! A First Lady should be a showman and a salesman, a clothes horse and a publicity sounding board, with a good heart and a real interest in the folks in 'Rising Star' and 'Rosebud,' as well as Newport and whatever the other fancy places are. Well, the last — real interest — I do have." [34]

One more meeting of her committee remained before the conference. It took place on the USS *Sequoia* and involved a cruise on the Potomac. Earlier that same day, Mrs. Johnson presented beautification certificates to two Washington-area businesses for work they had done in supplying plants and landscaping assistance to schools and community centers in the city. At the dock the chair of the Citizens Council for a Clean Potomac gave her a litter bag like the ones that volunteers would use the following Sunday, 23 May, during Potomac Pick-up Day. The *Sequoia* then sailed. On the journey, Secretary Udall and other speakers talked about the river's history and its current pollution problems before the other committee members delivered the customary reports.

During the trip, Mrs. Johnson also announced the formation of a private fund-raising organization, the Society for a More Beautiful National Capital. Mary Lasker had agreed to serve as president, and there would be six trustees, including Carolyn Agger Fortas, the wife of Abe Fortas, as treasurer. Lasker knew that governmental money could not be used for many of the projects that the committee contemplated, and she wanted to tap the resources of those who were "rich and possibly sympathetic." Creating a private committee and securing its tax-exempt status took time; as a result, the group did not operate fully until 1966. Nonetheless, the initiative represented a further elaboration of Mrs. Johnson's program. As long as the society enjoyed the support and public endorsement of the First Lady, it raised substantial amounts of money for Washington.[35]

Mrs. Johnson's natural beauty campaign reached the highpoint of its opening phase when the White House Conference began on 24 May. The work of pulling the meeting together had gone forward ever since the Task Force on Natural Beauty had first suggested the idea in November 1964. Udall told the president in mid-January 1965 that "this conference will be meaningful to the American people if it inspires new action — and produces *new ideas* and *new solutions* to our conservation problems." To make the conference work, Udall added, would mean involving "the best minds in the country," and he suggested that Laurance Rockefeller should be the overall coordinator of the conference. By early February, Rockefeller had been so designated, which in turn led to the conversation that he and his wife had with the First Lady on 3 February about the conference and about conservation problems in general.[36]

Laurance Rockefeller had emerged as an important player in American conservation issues during the 1950s after a career in the aerospace industry. Long interested in the family's holdings in such projects as the Jackson Hole Preserve in Wyoming, he had taken part in evaluating the nation's resources for projects that linked conservation with defense needs. He also linked resort projects in Wyoming and the Virgin Islands with land donations to the National Park Service. Nathaniel Owings called him "a collector of exotic Shangri-las to be found in rare and beautiful locations where virgin powdered beaches and sparkling oceans met." In 1958 President Eisenhower had named Rockefeller as chair of the Outdoor Recreation Resources and Review Commission (ORRRC), which was to report back in three years on the state of the country's recreational resources and their anticipated use in the years ahead.[37]

The ORRRC's report, *Outdoor Recreation for America,* went to President Kennedy in January 1962. It predicted that outdoor recreation would triple by the year 2000 and declared that new approaches to the issue were imperative. One solution suggested recreation areas nearer to the cities because "the need is far more urgent close to home." The commission also recommended that a Bureau of Outdoor Recreation be established within the Interior Department. Rockefeller worked through the American Conservation Association, which he funded, to spread the message of the ORRRC during the early 1960s, spending almost $800,000 on the campaign. Kennedy then named Rockefeller to direct the Advisory Council on Recreation, and it was appropriate that he should also be a member of the Task Force on Natural Beauty in 1964.[38]

Rockefeller wanted to shape conservation policy, and his access to Lady Bird Johnson and the president enabled him to advance his view that beautification and good business were not in conflict. "Business should not regard this awakening of an appetite for natural beauty as unexpected or something novel or temporary," he told the Congress of American Industry in December 1965. Natural beauty "will turn out in the end to be just plain good business." His attitude mirrored many of the views that the Johnsons held in the same years, and it was natural that a working collaboration evolved.[39]

Rockefeller began organizing the conference in February 1965 with the assumption that the delegates should focus "on case histories of 'how to do it,'" taking examples of successful community action to promote natural beauty and learning from them. One problem that especially concerned Rockefeller was "effective intergovernmental relations," by which he apparently meant placing more authority in the Recreation Advisory Council to coordinate the federal government's activities on natural beauty. In mid-March, Rockefeller met with Lyndon Johnson in what a White House staff member dubbed a "really good On The Record" appointment that would command favorable news coverage for the announcement of the conference. The Johnsons both talked with Rockefeller during his visit, and the First Lady agreed that she would open the conference. The closing ceremonies would be at the White House, which Rockefeller believed would "lift this conference out of the ordinary and help it to claim the public attention we seek." [40]

Throughout March and April, requests to attend the conference flowed into the White House. Rockefeller said that in choosing panelists, he and his associate Henry L. Diamond emphasized "the individual, not the office." They sought a "cross section of varying points of view," a goal that required the careful selection of the fifteen panels of eight participants each. Three thousand people either applied or were nominated to attend the conference. Because the meeting would be held in the auditoriums of the Department of State and the Civil Service Commission, the number of those who could attend was limited to 800. From that group, Diamond and Rockefeller settled on the 120 people who would actually take part on the panels.[41]

Panelists were told that they were participating in a "hard" conference that sought "concrete, specific proposals for action, visionary or immediate." They were also asked to provide two-page summaries of what they planned to say. The initial submissions proved to be too vague and philosophical, and the organizers insisted on more focused presentations. On Sunday 23 May, closed sessions among the panelists provided the necessary direction and created what was later called a "constructive tension." [42]

Lady Bird Johnson opened the conference the next day. She did not record her thoughts about it in her published diary. In her remarks to the delegates she said that "in the catalogue of ills which afflicts mankind ugliness and the decay of our cities and countryside are high on America's agenda." She then posed the question to the group, "Can a great democratic society generate the concerted drive to plan, and having planned, to execute, the great projects

Lady Bird Johnson speaks at the Natural Beauty Conference, 24 May 1965.
(LBJ Library photograph, 34492)

of beauty?" Laurance Rockefeller followed her with comments that identified "the city, the countryside, and the highways" as the broad topics for scrutiny, and he urged his listeners to present "new, practical ideas for solving specific problems." They would not "solve all the problems of creating a beautiful America" in the thirty-six hours of the conference, but they could "take a big step—perhaps many steps—in that direction."[43]

The deliberations of the conference were extensive and passionate. When published, the discussions came to more than 700 pages of text to cover all that was said in public. Lady Bird Johnson moved from panel to panel, taking "copious" notes in her own shorthand as the discussions went forward. Occasionally the panelists noticed and remarked that the First Lady was in the audience. There was much for her to hear. From the Federal-State-Local Partnership through the use of Citizen Action, the panelists experienced "a whole college course in the American environment in two days." Some sessions sparked controversy. The Roadside Control panel revealed the sharp differences that separated advocates of billboard regulation from representatives of the outdoor advertising industry. Ian McHarg of the University of Pennsylvania warned the Landscape Action Program panel: "We cannot indulge the despoiler any longer. He must be identified for what he is, as one who destroys the inheritance of living and unborn Americans, an uglifier who is unworthy of the right to look his fellows in the eye—be he who he is—industrialist, merchant, developer, Christian, Jew or agnostic." There was also, as landscape architect Lawrence Halprin noted, "throughout the conference the continuing dichotomy between the feeling that beauty must be equated with natural beauty and that manmade events are inherently ugly."[44]

On the afternoon of 25 May the panel chairs made their recommendations to the conference delegates. Then everyone assembled on the White House lawn, on what Henry Diamond recalled as "a hot, humid May afternoon." Rain washed out the plans to have the president hear some of the reports near the south portico. Instead, Johnson beckoned to everyone: "You all come inside." In the East Room, with most of the delegates sitting on the floor, the chairs of four panels gave brief digests of the reports to the president. "Natural beauty, as you and I conceive it," Lyndon Johnson responded, "is the world we live in. It is the environment in which we were born, and grow to maturity, and live our lives." In rambling remarks, which referred to his responsibilities in Vietnam and the Dominican Republic, the president added that he was sometimes awakened from his afternoon naps "by Lady Bird and Laurance Rockefeller and others in the next room, talking about flowers, roadsides and so forth." That afternoon, as he awoke, he had heard conversations and said, " 'My! Am I dreaming? Is Laurance Rockefeller back in town again?' And I got up and went out and pulled the curtain and peeped behind it and looked, and there was not only Laurance Rockefeller and Lady Bird and the sixty that started out with them but a thousand more that joined them." On a more substantive note, he promised that his next State of the Union message would contain beautification recommendations. He planned to call local and regional conferences on natural beauty, and he would transmit the proposals of the conference for state and local action to appropriate officials at those levels. He then announced that the next day Congress would receive a package of four bills dealing with the beautification of the nation's highways, including billboard control. "I thought that you would be glad to know that we have not been idle while you have been working," he told them.[45]

The Johnsons were proud of the Natural Beauty Conference and its work. The First Lady called it "an occasion of inspiration and brilliance," and she believed that "all of us who attended feel renewed in our dedication to the enhancement of the cities and communities in which we live." In an architectural journal, one observer called the conference "well organized and well run," and labeled it "on the whole a great success. It came forth with no new great solutions; many platitudes were passed around; an occasional bright and shining new idea came through." *National Wildlife* reported that Lady Bird Johnson was becoming "an unofficial 'secretary of the exterior.' "[46]

Not all the aspects of the conference received uniform praise. The way in which the issue of highway beauty and billboard control was handled left some of the participants grumbling that the White House had yielded too much to the outdoor advertising industry. Members of garden clubs and roadside councils went away angry from the gathering. Nonetheless, the overall tone of the conference was favorable.

The conference marked an early climax of Mrs. Johnson's beautification drive. As Henry Diamond said nineteen years later, "The word went out from the White House that the President and the First Lady cared." The conference served as a constructive catalytic

event that provided a national impetus to the conservation and
beautification policies of the Johnson years. In the two decades that
followed, Mrs. Johnson often encountered individuals who told her,
"with a sense of comrades in arms, 'I was at the White House Conference on Natural Beauty.'" [47]

The conference also occurred around the time when the Johnson
presidency was moving away from the euphoric optimism of the
1964 election and the early months of 1965, when legislative progress
toward the Great Society seemed inevitable. At the Conference on
Natural Beauty there were no protests about Vietnam and almost
no sense of the social turmoil that soon enveloped Johnson's administration. Within three weeks at the White House Festival of the
Arts in mid-June, protests from some of the guests about the war
signaled that a new and more difficult phase was beginning for the
Johnsons and the nation.

For Lady Bird Johnson the first half of 1965 had seen the beautification campaign launched, with a highly positive public response.
National legislation to improve highway beauty went to Congress
on 26 May 1965 with reasonable prospects of success, in the White
House's view. The First Lady's committee had captured the imagination of many people in Washington; volunteers and contributions
were still flowing in. It remained for her to implement her programs
in the capital city, where she would have to balance the desires of
those who wished to beautify the monumental and tourist areas of
Washington with the ideas of those who believed that beauty should
also be spread among the residents of the inner-city ghetto.

CHAPTER 4

BEAUTIFYING THE TWO WASHINGTONS

Lady Bird Johnson's beautification effort in Washington, DC developed along two complementary lines between 1965 and 1969. The first, identified with Mary Lasker and Nash Castro, looked to improvements in the appearance of the city in areas where tourists were most prevalent and the buildings most monumental. Their work overlapped to some extent with Nathaniel Owings's campaign to revitalize Pennsylvania Avenue. Mrs. Johnson also sought to secure an art museum for Washington by persuading Joseph Hirshhorn to donate his collection of art to the nation.

The second approach grew from the commitment of Walter Washington and Polly Shackleton to the residents of the inner city. Washington and Shackleton believed that beautification must make an active appeal to the sympathies of the African-American population. Katie Louchheim styled the Lasker-Castro group as the "daffodil and dogwood" set in contrast to Walter Washington's ghetto-oriented concern with schools, playgrounds, and housing projects. It was never that simple, but the broad tendencies were real.[1]

Lady Bird Johnson knew that success in the nation's capital depended on her ability to gain favorable publicity for her campaign. To achieve changes in the way that Washington looked, she had to capitalize on the natural curiosity about presidents' wives, and she had to tie that popular interest to beautification. Her emphasis on how to make monumental Washington look better was a first step toward addressing the issue of enhancing the city's appearance in less glamorous areas.

An indispensable aide to Lady Bird Johnson's work in Washington was Mary Lasker, who put her time, money, and hard work at the First Lady's disposal from 1965. She became the most important single force in the floral and monumental aspect of beautification in Washington. Born in 1900, she had made a successful business career in dress sales before she met Albert Lasker in 1939. He was a prominent advertising executive, and they found a common interest in medical research. "You will need *federal* money," Lasker told her; "what's more, I'll show you how to get it." They founded the Albert and Mary Lasker Foundation, which underwrote research on major disease through an annual awards program. Albert Lasker died of cancer in 1952 and his widow carried on his work. She placed her money with politicians who could advance her medical research goals. By the late 1950s, Mary Lasker had what amounted to a personally financed health lobby on Capitol Hill.[2]

Natural beauty claimed another part of Lasker's relentless energies. "Flowers in a city are like lipstick on a woman," she informed New York City officials. "You *have* to have some color." She planted flowers along the streets and sidewalks of New York City and had some twenty-six blocks under her supervision by 1960. "It's important in dollars and cents for a city to establish a pleasant image of itself," she said in 1960. Still, health issues were her main concern. "The flowers are just a side issue with me," she said in 1957; "I just hope that I am spark-plugging a movement that the city will carry on. What I am most interested in is the expansion of medical research." She kept the same priorities during the mid-1960s, and her combined commitment to health and beautification gave her a natural and reinforcing access to President and Mrs. Johnson. By pursuing both projects simultaneously, she ensured that her views would be heard on the medical issues that mattered to her. Thus, her work with Lady Bird Johnson was more than simple benevolence; it was a central component in the lobbying of an unsurpassed mover of the levers of power and influence in Washington.[3]

To some degree, Lasker used the First Lady for her own benevolent purposes. She made endless gestures of thoughtfulness and kindness, which were the price of ready access to the White House, to plead the case for medical research. There was no insincerity in Lasker's concern for beauty, but there was no innocence either. Yet influence and use did not run in a single direction; Mrs. Johnson gained as much from Mary Lasker as she gave her. The money and the time that Lasker spent on plantings, which ran into hundreds of thousands of dollars (several million in 1998 dollars), was largely responsible for the breadth of the beautification campaign in Washington. There would not have been a Society for a More Beautiful National Capital without Lasker. Considered only as a political exchange, and leaving out the real affection that the two women shared, the balance in the Lasker-Johnson transaction tilted heavily to the First Lady's side.

A key aide in the Johnson-Lasker program for Washington, DC was Nash Castro of the National Park Service. In 1965 he was the assistant regional director for administration within the National Capital Region. The forty-five-year-old Castro was a consummate public servant. He had the capacity to carry out efficiently the wishes of a First Lady when the resources of the National Park Service were needed, and he did so with discretion and good humor. Lady Bird Johnson soon came to regard him as "indispensable." The square-faced, wiry-haired Castro became a familiar part of Lady Bird Johnson's journeys about Washington, and his exertions helped to produce the successes that beautification achieved in recasting the look of the Federal District. "I continue to marvel at the depth of the First Lady's interest in the great work she has begun," Castro told his superiors in January 1966.[4]

The National Park Service and Mary Lasker were natural allies. They believed that money and manpower were best devoted to the parts of Washington that tourists visited and that governmental officials traveled through. Lasker's goal was to "plant masses of flowers where the masses pass." She was also convinced that it would be easier to persuade wealthy donors to provide funds for parks and gardens than for projects in the city's black districts. The Park Service emphasized the same set of implicit priorities. What it managed could be kept clean and tidy; what ghetto residents operated tended to deteriorate over time. Lasker and Castro did much for Washington and Lady Bird Johnson. If their social vision had limits, it was only on how best to involve the black community in the beautification cause.[5]

During 1965 Lady Bird Johnson, Lasker, and Castro evolved a working style that produced effective results for Washington. The First Lady spent time with them on frequent inspections trips through the city. While approving their plans to upgrade the areas where tourists were most concentrated, she also told them that "we must earnestly give attention to the development of tot lots and playgrounds, especially in the poorer sections of town." She addressed the look of the National Airport, the many traffic triangles in the city, and the places where plantings had become thin. Always, she cautioned her associates to "remember that we are using public funds to carry out these beautification projects" and to be "sure to use them wisely and well." The American people, Nash Castro decided, were fortunate "to have in the White House a First Lady of Mrs. Johnson's makeup, who so deeply loves her fellow human beings as to strive as assiduously as she does to enlarge the quality of their lives through the upgrading of the environment." In the end, Castro believed, "the upgrading of our environment will inevitably upgrade the American character."[6]

Throughout this work, the First Lady understood that her campaign could succeed only if the public knew of her activities. The press relations aspect of beautification was ever on her mind. The high point of 1965 in this respect came on 25 November when the American Broadcasting Company aired a one-hour television special, "A Visit to Washington with Mrs. Lyndon B. Johnson on Behalf of a More Beautiful Capital." The program looked at the splendor of the District of Columbia but also pointed to its accumulating environmental problems of pollution and decay. "Other generations have left us these monuments, this beauty which we admire," she said in her concluding statement. "What will we leave to those who come after us?" Stewart Udall wrote to her enthusiastically after the program: "What a radiant film—and a radiant narrator! Who knows, maybe your ripple will become a wave?"[7]

Private funding was central to the flexibility of her program, and Mary Lasker pushed ahead in 1965 with the organization of the Society for a More Beautiful National Capital. By midsummer the group had accumulated $25,000, and Mrs. Johnson decided that it was time for the money to be used. Her suggestion was to allocate $10,000 for the improvement of the approach to the city along its Southwest Freeway. In late September the fund-raising brochure, *For a More Beautiful Capital,* was released, and it brought in another $11,000 by the end of the year.

Mary Lasker was the financial backer of the society during the early years of its existence. She put in $70,000 of her own money to complete a donation for the same amount toward the $140,000 needed for the planting of cherry trees at Hains Point. Lasker also helped to enlist the support of a Washington donor, Rose Zalles, for a park site at E Street and Constitution Avenue to the tune of $100,000.

Mary Lasker courted the White House and the First Lady assiduously throughout 1966. She sent Mrs. Johnson an autographed letter of Thomas Jefferson to be part of the memorabilia collection that the First Lady was building up in the White House. A book on gardens in England, a decorated antique plate, and a camera were other gifts from Lasker. Her efforts in promoting English landscape architect and gardening writer Russell Page to Mrs. Johnson did not work out, but the attempt was another testament to Lasker's persistence and thoroughness in dealing with the First Lady.

By the end of 1966, Nash Castro reported to the First Lady that the Park Service would be planting more than .5 million bulbs around Washington during the following spring. Lasker's 100,000 plants and the work of the beautification campaign had already begun to make a difference in the city. An exultant Castro wrote to the White House that "spring 1967 promises to be mighty beautiful in Washington." Udall told a meeting of the First Lady's committee on 30 November that "Mrs. Johnson's program is showing the nation that we do not have to wait for the millennium or the construction of new clean-cut cities, but that here and now, in the 1960s, we can renew the old cities, and have new dimensions of beauty and delight."[8]

By early 1967, however, the financial and political constraints arising from the Vietnam War and a mood of economy in Congress impinged on beautification in Washington. In a report to the White House, Mary Lasker sought additional funding for beautification at all levels. She argued that the 1960s "will be known to historians as the decade of the conservationist and the beautifier, the years when

Americans decided to improve their environment. *President John-son has done more for the American environment than any President before him.*" She urged the administration to ask for more money, and she suggested that the president visit some park sites and urban centers to see what had been beautified. Lasker's idea came at a time when the president found travel around the nation more difficult because of the rising tempo of Vietnam War protests; her call for higher appropriations was also badly timed, given the administration's difficulties with Capitol Hill.[9]

During the first half of 1967 the beautification drive brought positive results, given the efforts of Lasker and Lady Bird Johnson in the previous year. Several hundred thousand daffodil bulbs flowered along Rock Creek and Potomac Parkway because of Lasker's benevolence. Other parts of Washington showed the same signs of floral excellence. Behind the scenes, however, the problem of cost persisted. There were 9,000 vacant spaces for street trees in Washington. At a cost of $100 to plant one tree, $900,000 (almost $5 million in 1998 dollars) was the minimum amount needed at a time when the Park Service budget for tree planting was half that. Castro also noted somewhat ruefully that the Washington business community had been slow to participate in the effort. They were, he said, "among the greatest benefactors of our work and the ones who least support it."[10]

To make the campaign work, the ultimate resource was government money. Lasker went before the subcommittee of the House Appropriations Committee in mid-March to request "proper maintenance funds for the Park Service." She told the panel that the service "simply cannot stretch the budget to do the kind of job needed to be done." Through Lasker's efforts the administration endorsed more money for the Park Service.[11]

The accomplishment proved timely, because later in the summer unexpected congressional resistance to appropriating money for beautification flared. Congresswoman Julia Butler Hansen (D-WA) issued a statement in mid-August that she would "not authorize funds for beautification projects when money is urgently needed for essential programs." Hansen said that she could not approve a request from Interior to beautify Walt Whitman Park in the District because the $340,000 could be better spent on projects "which will provide badly needed housing, jobs, and playground facilities."[12]

Hansen's edict, if carried out, "seriously compromises our beautification objectives," Castro and Liz Carpenter told the First Lady on
29 August 1967. The Park Service would have to decline a gift from
Lasker of trees worth $200,000 because funds would not be available
for planting them. In the case of the Walt Whitman Park project,
$163,000 from the Associated General Contractors would also have
to be turned down. To the congresswoman's point about funds for
the ghetto, Castro and Carpenter pointed out that $1.127 million had
been spent "in depressed neighborhoods" over the preceding three
years, as compared with $845,000 in other areas of Washington.[13]

The Park Service opened negotiations with Hansen that at-
tempted to have the beautification funds reprogrammed so that the
gifts could be accepted. Lady Bird Johnson helped matters along
as well. During a trip through the Midwest in September 1967, she
commented positively on the virtues of small-town America. These
remarks led Hansen to write Lyndon Johnson, praising the First
Lady and making the case for breaking up "our ghettos in the cities
and redistribut[ing] some of our population into the rural areas of
America." Hansen pointedly noted that she hoped all governmental installations would not be located in large cities; she especially
wanted to see a federal hospital in her district. The White House
staff passed the letter on to Mrs. Johnson, who in turn wrote to
Hansen about her beautification experiences. The letter grouped
the congresswoman with "far-sighted leaders" who could "keep the
whole effort moving." Despite this timely stroking from the First
Lady, Hansen had not changed her policy position on beautification funds.[14]

Hansen held her ground when the director of the Park Service,
George B. Hartzog Jr., appeared before her panel in March 1968. She
pressed the director on whether the service's request for money to
do District landscaping had bowed to her wishes. "You don't have
Walt Whitman Park in this, have you?" she asked. Hartzog replied,
"No, I don't have it in there. I got the message." Hansen's insistence that fewer funds go for such projects, coupled with the need to
honor her social priorities as a powerful chair of an influential committee, limited what the Park Service could accomplish in 1968.[15]

Even Hansen had to concede, however, that the Park Service had
had an impact on the District in achieving beautification. Hartzog
laid out for the record the eighty park sites, the thirty-nine public

schools, and the eight playgrounds that had been landscaped. The number of flowers and bulbs that had been planted under Castro and Lasker's aegis ran into the millions. Hansen acknowledged that the appearance of Washington had "improved a thousand percent within the eight years I have been here," and she noted that it was particularly true when "you have the chrysanthemums and the azaleas in bloom."[16]

These positive results occurred because of the unstinting efforts of Mary Lasker and others who worked during 1967 and 1968 to carry on the planting campaign. They emphasized the planting of shade trees, again largely in the more affluent areas of the city, however. Lady Bird Johnson tried in various ways to nudge Lasker and her allies to include trees for "school grounds, housing projects, barren neighborhood streets, and long avenues," all of which "would benefit from this effort." Apparently, Mrs. Johnson's persuasive powers did not move Lasker, and the First Lady had to find other means to deal with beautification in the ghetto.[17]

While Lady Bird Johnson was working with Lasker and her own committee, she also devoted time to other aspects of the monumental appearance of Washington. In the case of the acquisition of the Joseph Hirshhorn art collection and the creation of the Hirshhorn Museum, her role was significant. She played an even more important part in the effort of Nathaniel Owings to rehabilitate Pennsylvania Avenue as part of the city's culture and commerce.

Joseph Hirshhorn had begun to look for a museum to house his huge collection of modern art and sculpture during the early 1960s. By 1964 he was talking with S. Dillon Ripley, secretary of the Smithsonian Institution, about building a Hirshhorn Museum on the Mall in Washington as a location for the entire collection. Presidential influence was central to Ripley's idea, and he decided to work through Lady Bird Johnson. The First Lady hoped to obtain a painting by Thomas Eakins for the White House collection, and Ripley told Liz Carpenter that Hirshhorn possessed thirty-two works by Eakins. Ripley also let Hirshhorn know about the First Lady's interest. "Mrs. Johnson is herself keenly aware of the importance of your collection to the nation," Ripley wrote to Hirshhorn.[18]

During 1965 the White House and Hirshhorn negotiated the terms of the prospective gift of his collection. Lady Bird Johnson became a central means of reassuring the mercurial benefactor. She visited the Hirshhorn home in August 1965 and downplayed her own knowledge of Impressionism and other art to let her host shine. When she arrived, she said to Hirshhorn, "I really know nothing about art. I'm prepared to learn." Her comments, which minimized the real extent of her expertise, suitably impressed Hirshhorn. "That was honest," he told his biographer, "and I respected her." The First Lady had not lost her understanding, gained first in East Texas, that men were uncomfortable with women whose intelligence and learning equaled or exceeded their own. Mrs. Johnson's tact helped further the talks with Hirshhorn that culminated in an official announcement of his gift on 17 May 1966. As Ripley said, "Mrs. Johnson was the decisive factor. Hirshhorn is crazy about her and the president."[19]

It took almost a decade to get the Hirshhorn Museum constructed. Congress approved the site in fall 1966 and, after further controversy about the location, groundbreaking ceremonies occurred on 9 January 1969, just before the Johnsons left Washington. The museum was dedicated more than five years later, and Mrs. Johnson then told reporters, "The fact of its being in the nation's capital is very special to me." She had reason to be proud of what she and President Johnson had done to bring Hirshhorn, his collection, and his museum to Washington.[20]

Other Washington projects to which Lady Bird Johnson devoted her abundant energies were the campaigns to revitalize Pennsylvania Avenue and the Mall. She worked closely with Stewart Udall and Nathaniel Owings to bring these two endeavors to completion, and her "charm and serenity" were exercised at decisive points to shape the projects. What Owings called the First Lady's "gentle urgency" was behind both aspects of the effort to improve the monumental center of the city.[21]

John Kennedy had begun to address the future of Pennsylvania Avenue during his administration, forming the President's Council on Pennsylvania Avenue, with Owings as chair after 1 June 1962. With the help of the young Daniel Patrick Moynihan, Owings sought to provide a special character for "the nation's ceremonial way." By the time of President Kennedy's death, the council's plan was ready to be presented to Congress.[22]

While the plans for the avenue were pending in the early days of the Johnson administration, Mrs. Johnson met with Owings in May 1964; they "discussed open spaces and flower beds," which "tied in with the Pennsylvania Avenue plan." It was a year later, however, before the president set up a Temporary Commission on Pennsylvania Avenue by executive order, with Owings again as its chair. By this time Owings was also a member of the First Lady's Committee. A close collaboration among Lady Bird Johnson, Udall, and Owings ensued. On one occasion, she, Owings, and Udall were "sitting on the floor of Lady Bird's sitting room studying a great long drawing rolled across the carpet, Stewart squatting at one end, [Owings] at the other, and Lady Bird in the middle." At that point, President Johnson walked in and said, "What in hell, Udall, are you doing there on the floor with my wife?" [23]

Owings unveiled his overall plan for the Mall when Mrs. Johnson's committee met on 24 September 1965. "The central area of Washington should be the image of our country in the tradition of America," he told them. After hearing the plans, the First Lady added that her main hope was to see "some little gem completed within two or three years because it would give evidence to the public, and make them want to see the long completion of it." President Johnson asked Congress on 30 September to declare Pennsylvania Avenue a historic site and to create a Permanent Commission on Pennsylvania Avenue.[24]

The joint resolution to establish the commission reached Capitol Hill during spring 1966 and there it encountered political difficulties. Conflicts over other projected monuments and the John F. Kennedy Center for the Performing Arts slowed the process, as did the opposition of the ranking minority member on the House Committee on Interior and Insular Affairs, John Saylor (R-PA). As these problems mounted, Owings and Udall turned to Lady Bird Johnson for political support. Udall told Liz Carpenter that "the First Lady should be personally identified with the master plan for the Great Central Mall." Her endorsement was a significant asset that Owings and Udall coveted. Her help became particularly important when the resolution halted on Capitol Hill. As the end of the congressional session approached in fall 1966, Owings obtained Mrs. Johnson's agreement to push the measure. Nonetheless, Saylor's opposition prevented action until 1967.[25]

The same alignment of opposing forces stalled the resolution in 1967. Mrs. Johnson indicated her support for the commission both publicly and privately, but the clout that she enjoyed with Congress could not overcome the enmity of Saylor and others toward Owings and his plans. The administration made concessions to Saylor during 1968, but it was not enough. Not until October 1972, under Richard Nixon, did a Pennsylvania Avenue bill finally emerge from Congress in a form that Owings accepted. Nevertheless, the First Lady and the architect had helped Pennsylvania Avenue and its related project of the Mall pass through the difficult first phase of what became a two-decade process of revitalization. The architect later wrote of Lady Bird Johnson that she "provided the leadership that changed the political climate in Washington to being favorable to aesthetic considerations, through her personal participation in a positive program." Unlike her husband, who was suspicious of Pennsylvania Avenue as a Kennedy project, Lady Bird Johnson grasped the cultural significance of what the avenue could represent as a model for other cities, and she made a decisive contribution to the ultimate success of the project.[26]

Despite her good work with monumental Washington, Lady Bird Johnson knew that if her beautification efforts were confined to that part of the capital, they would be flawed and incomplete. From the outset of her campaign she recognized that the inner city and its black neighborhoods had to be an essential part of her priorities. Through Walter Washington, Polly Shackleton, and other supporters, Mrs. Johnson took beautification into the ghetto and, as Washington put it, "went to the heart of filling the gap and beginning to work with the alienation" of the city's black residents.[27]

From the formation of the First Lady's Committee for a More Beautiful Capital, there was a consensus among the participants that a beautification strategy had to be directed at the urban problems of Washington. "It is not enough to have a showcase, even the most beautifully designed and landscaped cultural center," wrote Antonia Chayes in December 1964; "these human expressions must be made relevant to everyone, or they are as inaccessible as if they were miles away."[28]

The question, of course, was how to accomplish these goals in a manner that would affect the black neighborhoods of Washington in a positive way. The first step was to recruit at least one black member for the committee to provide links with the inner city. In 1965 there were only a few blacks whose careers had given them enough visibility to come to Lady Bird Johnson's attention. The name that popped up frequently was Walter Washington, the executive director of the National Capital Housing Authority since 1961.

Approaching his fiftieth birthday, Washington was a Georgia native who had grown up in Jamestown, New York. Marriage to Bennetta Bullock, the daughter of a prominent Washington clergyman, made him part of the network of influential black families in the city. He had worked on housing in the District since the 1940s. One of his black associates called him "a smooth briefcase operator who had learned the white man's game and was excellent at it." [29]

The First Lady's committee gave Walter Washington a way to improve the situation of some of the city's black residents, and he proceeded with his customary efficiency and persistence to take advantage of the chance. "I like to be judged on performance, and not on what somebody believes," he later said, and Mrs. Johnson discovered that his sensitivity and ingenuity also produced positive results. On 9 March 1965, at Washington's urgings, she included the Greenleaf Gardens Project in one of the tours of her committee. There "a small crowd of the neighborhood folks were gathered to greet us, including two school bands, which performed loudly and enthusiastically, if not perfectly." She made "a short speech, with little children wandering around," and called it "a good start, a good morning." [30]

With Washington as her guide, Mrs. Johnson ventured into the black neighborhoods during spring 1965, "where the conditions are gray and dismal," to see what her committee might accomplish. Washington recalled that she rarely missed any key details, and he knew that he had to be ready to respond to the items she noticed as they walked along and talked. Her readiness to plunge into even the most grim surroundings and her ease with the crowds that gathered left an enduring impression on him.

As shrewd politicians, Lady Bird Johnson and Walter Washington knew that publicity was key to the success of their campaign. When the First Lady received a letter from John Hatcher, a young black man who lived on Fiftieth Street, it offered her an opportunity to make a point about the direction of her work. "I would like for my yard to look more beautiful," Hatcher wrote. "If you would please send me azaleas, I will plant them. Then you would not have to come all the way out to 50th street to plant them for me."[31]

By this time Washington was ready to launch "a rather massive cleanup campaign" for the Forty-ninth Census Tract. The goal, he said, "was an attempt to motivate the children, youth, adults, and family units in a long-range program of self-involvement for enhancing the physical appearance of the community." Hatcher's letter fit right in with that drive.[32] The First Lady responded to the young Washingtonian that "we can keep our properties and school-grounds neat, we can pick up litter, but there are few things we can do that will bring more joy than the planting of fine flowers." Walter Washington also ensured that the delivery of an azalea bush to Hatcher's home was well covered by the local press.[33]

Washington pursued an ambitious summer agenda in 1965. Working with the District's school system, he identified a number of junior highs and elementary schools to experience pilot beautification plantings. Money from local businesses funded the installation of plants and trees through the work of neighborhood children and adult residents. During the summer, Washington pushed forward in the Forty-ninth Census Tract with his "clean-up, fix-up, paint-up, and plant-up" campaign. Howard University students and local volunteers pitched in as the Health Department hauled away sixty-five truckloads of trash from a single block. These activities continued into fall 1965. Lynda Johnson selected the John F. Cook School at 30 P Street, Northeast, and presented it with a check for $1,500 from her own funds for beautification.[34]

Although Washington's initial efforts were impressive, several influential members of the First Lady's Committee were looking for a greater emphasis on inner-city beautification. Katharine Graham of the *Washington Post* brought Washington, Katie Louchheim, and several other such proponents to her home for lunch "to try to pool our efforts, and perhaps even establish a series of priorities, in order to give more effective service" to Mrs. Johnson's campaign. The group proposed that the First Lady name a steering committee to act as "a central clearing house so to speak."[35]

The initiative grew out of Washington's realization that he did not have the staff resources and support that Lasker and Nash Castro had. Lady Bird Johnson was sympathetic to the sentiments that

Graham and Washington expressed, but she was not ready to turn the direction of her beautification drive over to a panel of her committee members. She responded politely to the suggestions, however.

Mrs. Johnson did demonstrate her personal interest in the District's local schools in order to support Washington's initiative. She went to a number of places, including Terrell Junior High. Outside Terrell, students from the nearby Perry School spotted the First Lady in her car. As they waved, "she lowered her car window and motioned them over. She shook hands with many of them and asked them all to be sure and tend the plants and otherwise look after them, to keep litter away from the area, and to protect the new windowpanes that [had] been installed at Terrell School." [36]

Walter Washington's hard work came up against the twin obstacles of a cumbersome city bureaucracy and a continuing absence of secure funding. He tried to overcome the first problem through his membership on an Inter-Agency Committee on Beautification Programs for the District, an appointment that had the First Lady's warm support. Even with this new post, Washington still found it difficult to move the local government to adopt beautification initiatives.

Private philanthropy remained key to Washington's success. Early in 1966, Brooke Astor enlisted in the First Lady's campaign for beautification of the district's school facilities. After touring the schools and housing projects, Astor, who had been generous in providing funds for such facilities in New York City, decided to concentrate on the Buchanan School. She pledged money to upgrade the school, materially assisting Washington's goals. Despite these successes, Washington was facing mounting difficulties in carrying forward his endeavor during winter 1966. He needed some help from within the committee, preferably from someone with political muscle and influence with Lady Bird Johnson. To that end, Katie Louchheim suggested that the Neighborhoods and Special Projects Committee be reconstituted to include four women who would provide citizen interest in beautification.

One of the names that Louchheim put forward had an immediate appeal to Lady Bird Johnson. Polly Shackleton had been on the First Lady's Committee since its inception. A resident of the District

Sharon Francis, Brooke Astor, Lady Bird Johnson, and Laurance Rockefeller
at the Buchanan School in Washington, DC, 17 January 1968.
(LBJ Library, Robert Knudsen photograph, C8199-7A)

since 1939, Shackleton had been a staff member at the American
Institute of Architects and a longtime Democratic party activist in
Washington. She wanted to build on what the First Lady had already
done as a means of expanding job training for ghetto youths. She
believed that an Operation Pride project could address the many
alleys and streets in the city that were "full of trash," and she sought
Mrs. Johnson's blessing to "try and come up with some suggestions
and recommendations." The First Lady responded that "nothing
would please me more than to see" the list of job-training projects
in the District expanded.[37]

Polly Shackleton and Walter Washington developed a more com-
prehensive program of employment opportunities for young black
men in summer 1966, which they called Project Pride. The Society
for a More Beautiful National Capital agreed to fund the proposal
with an initial grant of $7,000. With help from the National Capital
Housing Authority and Howard University students, the project got
under way, and eighty high-school students worked on it through
the Neighborhood Youth Corps.

Project Pride started first in mid-July 1966 in the Shaw School
urban renewal area. The press release quoted Mrs. Johnson as being

"delighted that the people in the Shaw area have taken the initiative in Project Pride and that private and governmental agencies are cooperating to make this demonstration project a success." Within a month, the work began to show results. Liz Carpenter remarked that "rat baiting, painting-up, etc." was "going full force" and represented "just the kind of thing needed to offset long hot summer situations."[38]

The positive achievements of Project Pride in 1966 were impressive. Some 250 children took part in rat baiting, removing trash, and home repairs. One of the area residents said, "Makes you feel better to walk around and see something so pretty." Another participant observed, "I sure hope you get bigger next year so you can clean up the whole city."[39]

The immediate problem was how to continue the campaign into 1967. As the *Washington Post* asked, "Will Pride Go Before the Fall?" Cutbacks in the District's budget in 1967 compelled Shackleton to turn to Laurance Rockefeller and other donors to underwrite the effort that she now called Project Trail Blazers. Looking ahead to 1967, Rockefeller warned that private funding could not go on forever. Such proved to be the case. President Johnson's withdrawal from the 1968 election and the rioting that followed the death of Martin Luther King Jr. dried up private and public sources of funding.[40]

The shift in political mood did not invalidate the work that Shackleton, Washington, and the First Lady had tried to do in Project Pride and Project Trail Blazers. Within the modest means available to them, they had done what they could to make beautification relevant to the inner city. They had endeavored to involve the residents themselves and not to dictate from above what should be done. These small-scale projects did not strike at the roots of Washington's racism, poverty, and urban decay; but neither did they stem from the easy view that until one could improve everything, the best course was to do nothing. As Walter Washington told a *National Geographic* writer during fall 1966, "When this program started, there were some, I suppose, who regarded it as Marie Antoinette's piece of cake. I mean, out in east Washington, how many rats can you kill with a tulip? But it hasn't been that way at all. We started with mass plantings, then moved on to Project Pride, and now here we are."[41]

Walter Washington's friendship with Lady Bird Johnson led to greater personal opportunities for him. In an effort to revitalize the District government after the failure to achieve home rule for the city in 1965, President Johnson sought, during summer 1966, to persuade Washington to become one of the three commissioners for the District. The sticking point was whether Washington would become president of the Board of Commissioners, replacing a white man. If he assumed the post, Washington would exercise responsibility over the city's police. In 1966, Lyndon Johnson, still attuned to southern sensibilities in Congress, did not want a black man in charge of the police force. Washington declined to accept Johnson's offer of the place of second commissioner, a post that a black man already held. Instead, Washington went to New York City as its housing commissioner in November 1966.

Nine months later, Congress had approved Lyndon Johnson's plan to reorganize the District's government, specifying a single commissioner or mayor in charge of the city. In the selection process, Mrs. Johnson kept reminding her husband that Walter Washington was the logical choice, and the president finally decided to appoint him. Although leaks threatened to derail the selection, Johnson finally sent in the nomination on 6 September 1967. He called Washington to talk about the job and said, "A good friend of yours is sitting here beside me, and she and I think there's important work for you [to] do down here." Just before the announcement of the nomination, Johnson told his choice, "Those gals who work for Bird in the East Wing sure like you, Walter." The nomination, which met with broad approval in the District and across the country, exemplified the personal credibility that Walter Washington had gained during his collaboration with the First Lady.[42]

Lady Bird Johnson's efforts to transform Washington included another ambitious project on which she embarked during the second half of 1966. She sponsored a sweeping effort to refurbish and rehabilitate the Capitol Hill area and other parts of the city under the auspices of her committee and the Society For a More Beautiful National Capital.

The initial impetus for the project came from an urban philanthropist and civil rights supporter, Stephen Currier. Married to a member of the Mellon family, Currier used his Taconic Foundation to pursue social change in the cities. In late 1965 he proposed to the

White House that a conference be held on Urban America, and the event was scheduled for September 1966. During discussions about Mrs. Johnson's role in the conference, Currier and Sharon Francis explored ways to enhance Mrs. Johnson's work in the District. While the conference took place, Francis developed some ideas for the First Lady's consideration.

Currier's scheme was to have a major landscape architect devise plans for vest-pocket parks or for the entire Anacostia waterfront. He and Francis also wanted to engage the services of Lawrence Halprin of San Francisco, designer of Ghirardelli Square. The First Lady toured the square during a swing through California in late September, and she told Francis to arrange a visit for Halprin in Washington.

Halprin toured the city on 13 October with Nash Castro, Polly Shackleton, and Walter Washington. In addition to his work at Ghirardelli Square, the fifty-year-old Halprin had attracted national attention for such projects as the Sea Ranch vacation community in California and for his ideas about the design of the Bay Area Rapid Transit System in San Francisco. As Halprin's ideas about Washington developed, Currier put up the money to engage the architect's services. Designs for improving neighborhoods in the East Capitol area and for creating recreation areas elsewhere in the District took shape. Meanwhile, Francis began working with the District bureaucracy on Halprin's behalf.

These threads came together when Halprin made a presentation to the First Lady's committee on 12 January 1967. He spoke of developing vest-pocket parks from vacant lots, transforming alleys into swimming pools or playgrounds, and building new freeways along the Anacostia River. "What people really want in an environment is what's going to solve their problems," Halprin told a reporter. "If living problems are solved, the chances are the environment will end up being beautiful."[43]

Halprin's proposals set off a spirited debate within the committee. Had his ideas gone forward in their original form, they might have sparked a lively controversy. However, the committee's sense of optimism about Halprin's suggestions lasted only five days. On 17 January Stephen Currier and his wife were lost on a flight from Puerto Rico to the Virgin Islands. As a result of their deaths, the momentum behind the Halprin initiative slowed dramatically. The control of the Taconic Foundation passed into other, less sympathetic hands.

Over the next two years, Sharon Francis worked hard to move the essence of the Halprin campaign through an increasingly resistant District bureaucracy and congressional appropriations process. Elaborate negotiations resulted in very little tangible accomplishment by January 1969.

Could the Currier-Halprin proposals ever have worked? Given sufficient time and a greater degree of commitment from Congress and the bureaucracy, they could have had a chance for success. Some observers around Lady Bird Johnson found Halprin impractical and his ideas difficult to sell. Yet his proposals offered some fresh thinking about the District's problems, and his ideas could have had a positive impact as demonstration projects. Once the initial impetus of the Currier gift disappeared, however, the Halprin concepts collided with the interests of the affected residents, the opposition of the Park Service and highway interests, and the growing disillusionment with the Johnson administration and all its policies. Nonetheless, Lady Bird Johnson's willingness to encourage Halprin and his plans showed that her definition of urban beautification was not a limited one.

By spring 1968 it was time for Lady Bird Johnson to look back on her work in Washington and see what it had meant to the city she had come to love. On Saturday, 30 March 1968, the day before her husband's surprise announcement that he would not be a presidential candidate, she went with Castro, Liz Carpenter, and a few reporters on an extended tour of the city's parks. As they walked through West Potomac Park and Hains Point and ate a picnic lunch, Mrs. Johnson turned to Castro and said, "It makes it all worthwhile, doesn't it, Nash?" During the remainder of the year the balance sheet on Lady Bird Johnson's efforts for Washington was calculated. The Society for a More Beautiful National Capital had raised more than $2.5 million for its work, hundreds of thousands of bulbs, trees, and plants had been added to the landscape, and the look of the city had been transformed.[44]

Within a week, however, the First Lady and the nation received a sobering reminder of the dimensions of the urban problems that

Lady Bird Johnson and Washingtonians in the city's parks, 29 March 1968.
(LBJ Library, Robert Knudsen photograph, C9275-15A)

the nation faced. After the murder of Martin Luther King Jr. on
4 April 1968, the black residents of the city poured into the streets
and began to burn businesses, loot other stores, and riot throughout
the heart of the ghetto. Lady Bird Johnson was at the White House
when the news of the assassination came, and for her "the evening
assumed a nightmare quality." [45]

After a previously planned trip to Texas, the First Lady returned to Washington on 10 April. During her absence, Bess Abell had told her about "the incessant barrage of TV coverage . . . of lootings and fires. It had been as though I were talking to the inhabitant of another planet." When she surveyed the damage to Washington, the First Lady was gratified that many of the places she had sought to beautify had been spared in the rioting. "One would like to assume that these beautiful spots meant so much that people didn't want to harm them," Sharon Francis recalled, "and that can be at least in part true." [46]

At a meeting of her committee on 17 April, Lady Bird Johnson told the group, "This has been one of the most lovely springs I can remember in Washington's history. It has also been one of the most poignant and grave. That fact underscores the urgency of improving the environment for all people." [47]

Mrs. Johnson then introduced Walter Washington, who responded to her remarks with a moving statement that looked back on the committee's record and her part in it. It was, Sharon Francis said, "his charismatic kind of performance where he started out with tears coming down his face." To those who labeled beautification as "cosmetic," the mayor replied, "You cannot tell me that the neighborhood in Greenleaf Housing Project in Southeast, when hundreds of people came out, painted, fixed up their neighborhoods and said 'we would like to be part of this' is cosmetic." In closing, Washington said, "The greatest thing that we can do for the greatest First Lady I have ever known is to dedicate ourselves to continue with this great work." Lady Bird Johnson sat there as the mayor said "so many kind, warm, generous things about me that I began to shrink down and look at my plate." Still it was for her "a great climax to three years of hard work together." [48]

In the inner city, the First Lady had expended her time and resources on the Shaw neighborhood, for Anacostia, and the Trail Blazers and Project Pride. She had not, of course, affected the intrinsic ills of the city and its black ghetto, a task that was beyond the scope of her campaign. Nonetheless, she had addressed these issues with the means available to her. Walter Washington was right that the First Lady had made a difference to the lives of the District's residents.

Washington had also been correct in his 17 April speech when

Walter Washington and Lady Bird Johnson, 3 November 1967.
(LBJ Library, Frank Wolfe photograph, C7266-25)

he recalled John Hatcher's first letter to Mrs. Johnson in 1965: "The First Lady sent a plant out there. The result was that a little boy would be reborn; a neighborhood and a school were electrified and the community moved into action." Her willingness to respond to the John Hatchers of the 1960s in Washington reflected the First Lady's commitment to a broad definition of beautification that had room for Mary Lasker and Polly Shackleton, for Nash Castro and Walter Washington.[49]

Decades after she left Washington, Lady Bird Johnson's influence on the city remained. When she received a gold medal from Congress in 1984, the support that flowed in from friends in Washington sounded a recurrent theme. "Through her and her committee's work," wrote Elizabeth Rowe, "Washington bloomed as it never had before. And it is still blooming." Every spring in Washington, as the cherry trees blossom on Hains Point and flowers appear in the parks and along the roadways, the collective thought in the city is "thank God for Lady Bird Johnson."[50]

In assessing the contributions of First Ladies to American life, judgments often adopt male-centered criteria to evaluate what these women have accomplished. When Lady Bird Johnson beautified the monumental areas of Washington and addressed the difficult problems of inner-city life at the same time, she was engaging in a campaign that, had a man pursued it, would have been regarded as a significant contribution to urban life in a major city. Her record in the White House becomes even more impressive when her efforts to beautify Washington are placed beside her other drive to improve the nation's highways and the landscape through which they ran. Her sponsorship and implementation of the Highway Beautification Act of 1965 were yet another indication of how significant her performance as First Lady was during the 1960s.

CHAPTER 5

BEAUTIFYING
THE HIGHWAYS

The national environmental legislation with which Lady Bird Johnson is most identified is the Highway Beautification Act of 1965. Called Lady Bird's bill at the time, the measure surfaces whenever the issue of unsightly billboards and junk yards is raised. In the three decades since its enactment, the law has been so weakened as to make it virtually useless in restricting outdoor advertising. Critics in the environmental movement have charged that the law gave "the billboard companies custody of America the Beautiful." In fairness to the First Lady, however, she did the best that she could with what was politically possible at the time.[1]

When she took up the cause of controlling junkyards and billboards in late 1964, Lady Bird Johnson was entering an area of American politics where all the advantages lay with the outdoor advertising industry. Ever since billboards had first appeared, with the rise of the automobile at the turn of the century, opponents of outdoor advertising had endeavored to regulate these road signs with indifferent success. Some states and territories, such as Hawaii and Vermont, had imposed tight controls and kept their roads scenic. In most of the nation, however, regulation was lax. A few states accepted the contention that localities could control billboards by requiring owners to remove them. The billboard operators were given a fixed amount of time to recover their costs, and then the signs had to come down. Yet across most of the country, the industry, with its timely contributions to candidates and campaigns, had the upper hand as the 1950s ended.

In the drive against billboards, women had constituted a major element of the opposition for more than a half a century. State roadside councils and garden clubs were the primary means by which women interested in the appearance of highways made their influence felt on local governments. These groups, however, had not joined together into an effective national body by the 1960s. Accordingly, the billboard industry stereotyped them as self-appointed advocates of parochial and impractical "women's" attitudes in billboard battles. "We are not just a group of starry-eyed billboard fighters," said one leader of the roadside council movement at the Natural Beauty Conference. "We are just volunteers trying to fight for the beauty of our country." These women were a potential political resource of real value, but they lacked the visible muscle of the billboard lobby. The denigration of women as advocates of regulating outdoor advertising was one of the major obstacles that Lady Bird Johnson confronted in her own battle for highway beautification.[2]

The construction of the interstate highway system during the Eisenhower administration raised the stakes for the opponents of billboards. Congress agreed in the 1958 highway bill to grant states an extra .5 percent of federal-aid highway funds (the so-called "bonus" approach) if they controlled billboards, but that was as far as lawmakers wanted to go toward regulation. There was clear popular support for regulating billboards in general. Women's groups, especially the numerous roadside councils, rallied opinion in favor of controls. The industry countered that these groups were advancing parochial and impractical answers to the problem and that removal would deprive motorists of needed information and of diversion.

The billboard industry exercised great influence in Congress. Politicians needed billboards for their reelection campaigns. Businesses that depended on tourism favored outdoor advertising. Organized labor made up an additional and powerful part of the probillboard coalition. Workers who constructed, painted, and maintained the signs joined with other union members who worked in motels, restaurants, and other businesses to make the AFL–CIO a strong advocate of the industry's position.

The billboard lobby was attentive to lawmakers who might be helpful in opposing regulatory legislation and watchful for bills directed against its interests. Proponents of regulation could not match this array of political power; their best arguments were intangible. They said that a billboard-free roadway was better for the traveler's peace of mind. Scenic beauty should also be kept free from the clutter of unsightly signs. The constituency for natural beauty at the roadside was thus large but diffuse and difficult to mobilize. As a result, a bill to regulate billboards had to be limited and politic to survive in Congress.

As a senator, Lyndon Johnson did not spend much time on billboard issues, but he appears to have been sensitive to the power of the industry. He opposed the bonus bill in 1958, and a year later he supported a law that exempted from federal control all areas that had been zoned for business use before the bonus law went into effect. The Outdoor Advertising Association of Texas praised Johnson for having been "most helpful in the passage of this act" and applauded him for having "consistently opposed this trampling of people's rights." The spokesmen for the industry also remembered that Johnson had authorized the Democrats to spend a good deal of money on billboards in the 1964 presidential contest.[3]

By the time Johnson became president, momentum was growing for more stringent billboard control. Books such as Peter Blake's *God's Own Junkyard* (1964) aroused public concern about the deterioration of the landscape. "There are presently some 800,000 miles of federally aided highways in the United States," Blake wrote, "and the billboard lobby is permitted to deface every blessed mile of them." *Reader's Digest* and other periodicals called for stronger laws that went beyond the Bonus Act of 1958 and the timid steps that had occurred during the 1950s.[4]

The Natural Beauty Task Force saw billboard regulation and highway beauty as part of its charge. Reporting to the president in late November 1964, the task force advocated stringent control over billboards, including more coverage of primary and secondary roads that received federal aid; raising the bonus to the states to 2 percent; and creating scenic areas along the interstate system where no billboards would be allowed. In keeping with the president's instructions to leave the politics to him, the panel did not provide a strategy for enacting such an ambitious program.

Lady Bird Johnson became an open advocate of highway beauty in late 1963 or early 1964. She had driven yearly from Texas to Washington when her husband was in the House and Senate, and she had campaigned across her own state in the 1950s. As she did so, she noticed the increasing number of junkyards filled with abandoned automobiles. These experiences helped crystallize her concern about highway beautification. A few days after the 1964 election, the president called his secretary of commerce Luther Hodges and said, "Lady Bird wants to know what you're going to do about all those junkyards along the highways." The Commerce Department, the president told him, should come up with a program for highway beautification. The First Lady's interest galvanized the president, whose heightened sensitivity, in turn, claimed the attention of the bureaucracy in the White House and in the Department of Commerce.[5]

The Bureau of Public Roads reported that the government had the power to screen the 16,000 junkyards in the nation to improve scenic corridors. The more difficult task would be controlling billboard advertising along the interstate highway system. Commerce recommended that the 1958 law be extended and that states be required to control outdoor advertising and junkyards, lest they lose federal highway aid funds. If pursued in Congress, this program would pit the Johnson administration against the billboard lobby on Capitol Hill.

To get the bill that his wife wanted enacted into law, Lyndon Johnson and his aides determined on a risky but workable strategy. He planned to divide the outdoor advertising industry by attracting the owners of billboards in urban areas with concessions in the proposed law. Billboard owners in rural areas would thus be left on the sidelines and presumably unable to stop the legislation. Johnson no doubt realized that in a direct confrontation with the billboard lobby he would lose. He knew the political strength of the billboard and highway-construction coalition, both of which would be targets of laws that devoted money to removing billboards, cleaning up junkyards, and improving roadside landscapes. This divide-and-

conquer approach required, however, that the White House compromise with a key element of the industry and ignore the antibillboard supporters. Presumably, they would have to endorse some
billboard legislation as better than none at all. This assumption
turned out to be a crucial flaw in the antibillboard campaign.

During the first four months of 1965, the administration, led by
the influential White House aide Bill Moyers, worked out an arrangement in which billboards would be allowed in commercial and
industrial areas in return for the agreement of the Outdoor Advertising Association of America (OAAA), the main lobbying arm of
the urban billboard owners, to accept the exclusion of such advertising from scenic areas along interstate highways and the federally supported primary road system. Moyers conducted these talks
with the leading lobbyist for the OAAA, the lawyer Phillip Tocker.
Tocker saw this initiative from the White House as a way of securing
specific advantages for his members under the guise of accepting
regulation. Knowing relatively little about the technicalities of the
billboard industry, Moyers was not an equal match for the wily and
well-informed Tocker.[6]

In public, the president helped the antibillboard campaign get
under way during the early part of 1965. In his State of the Union
message on 4 January, Johnson said that "a new and substantial
effort must be made to landscape highways to provide places of re-
laxation and recreation wherever our roads run." On 21 January the
White House released a presidential letter to the secretary of commerce outlining Johnson's ideas about roadsides. The president did
not mention billboards but did discuss junkyards.[7]

Meanwhile, Lady Bird Johnson made clear in her public and private statements her intention to improve the appearance of highways. In her *U.S. News* interview in late February, she said that
"public feeling is going to bring about regulation, so that you don't
have a solid diet of billboards on the roads." She kept the OAAA
at arm's length but was cordial to advocates of control in the letters that went out from her office. "Preservation of this land's scenic
heritage is of great importance to me," she wrote, and she promised
to pay careful attention to the issue of "the elimination of unsightly
billboards." The First Lady and her staff did not, however, reach any
kind of working arrangement with antibillboard groups.[8]

During discussions in winter and spring 1965, the OAAA, the White House, and Commerce hammered out a series of billboard laws for submission to Congress. When the proposals came before the lawmakers in mid-April, the measures encountered a decidedly tepid response from the politicians who had to face unhappy billboard owners in their districts. As one White House aide said after hearing from lawmakers, "The billboard thing would be tough but not impossible."[9]

In the end, the White House and the OAAA found common ground on billboard legislation that was favorable to the industry. Billboards would be banned "except in those areas of commercial and industrial use," which represented a major loophole for billboard operators. They simply had to persuade states and localities to change their zoning laws to designate areas industrial or commercial, and billboards would be permitted. The industry also hoped that Congress would require the federal government and the states to compensate billboard owners when their signs were taken down, thus shifting removal costs from the billboard owners to the government and the taxpayers. By the time the White House Conference on Natural Beauty convened in May 1965, the White House and the industry were in agreement on the kind of billboard legislation that should be pursued.

Because they were not aware of the degree to which the administration had already collaborated with industry lobbyists, the members of the roadside-control panel at the conference recommended a law that would have banned billboards even in commercial areas. Then to the surprise of the panelists and the friends of billboard regulation, Lyndon Johnson, addressing the delegates, advocated the banning of billboards and junkyards from highways "except in those areas of commercial and industrial use." Their feelings slighted, the members of garden clubs, roadside councils, and other environmentally oriented groups withdrew their backing from the bills that went to Capitol Hill on 27 May. They would have been even angrier had they known that Phillip Tocker was at the White House that afternoon sitting in Moyers's office and listening to Johnson's speech.[10]

Highway beautification had the backing of Lyndon and Lady Bird Johnson. What it did not have was grassroots enthusiasm from the proponents of billboard control. It also faced the united opposition of billboard owners in rural areas, of the economic interests that depended on tourist travel and the signs that attracted motorists, and, most important, of lawmakers who were indebted to local billboard operators for campaign help. The proposed bills were known collectively as Lady Bird's bill, but to succeed the package needed all the president's power and the sizable Democratic majorities in Congress.[11]

With the bills in trouble, Lady Bird Johnson became involved in the legislative process as no First Lady before her had been. She kept up with the legislative situation in midsummer through information from Lawrence O'Brien, the administration's link with Congress, and she participated in a decision to drop some parts of the program that lacked support on Capitol Hill in mid-August. She also met with Walter Reuther, president of the United Auto Workers, to help him assemble votes for highway beauty. Mrs. Johnson told him, "We'll keep our fingers crossed about the beautification legislation. I've lived through enough last days of congressional sessions to know that anything can happen. We'll hope for the best!"[12]

The Johnsons did more than rely on hope in late summer 1965. The White House let it be known that "the highway beauty bill was one of the ones the president wanted this year, that he had to have this one . . . 'for Lady Bird.' " A participant in one of the strategy sessions in October recalled that Johnson said to his cabinet and staff, "You know I love that woman and she wants that Highway Beautification Act," and "by God, we're going to get it for her."[13]

The crucial part of Lady Bird Johnson's activity on behalf of the measure began on 11 September. By then the administration had broken with the Outdoor Advertising Association and was seeking, in the House version of the bill, to secure stronger language that would give the secretary of commerce a greater voice in the regulation of billboards. The situation in the House looked uncertain for billboard legislation. To move minds and votes on Capitol Hill, a working group met with President Johnson that Saturday afternoon. Lady Bird Johnson joined Lawrence O'Brien, Horace Busby, Douglass Cater, and ten other men as specific lobbying decisions were made. Participation in a legislative strategy session represented a departure for a First Lady. Not even Eleanor Roosevelt had sat in on such meetings, nor had she been given assignments to woo votes in Congress. Once again, Lady Bird Johnson was stretching the boundaries of what First Ladies could do.

She was assigned four House members to call personally, including the chair of the crucial subcommittee, John C. Kluczynski. The congressman owned a restaurant, and the president suggested that the call might find him "slapping mayonnaise" on bread. Lady Bird Johnson reached Kluczynski that afternoon, and a White House aide reported that "obviously Mrs. Johnson's call has had its effect and the Congressman is all for anything we want." Though Mrs. Johnson's lobbying work was helpful, the administration was at this point in direct opposition to the OAAA and to Phillip Tocker, who disliked what had been done to strengthen the bill.[14]

The highway beautification bill passed the Senate five days later. Significant changes had occurred in the measure on the floor that reduced its effectiveness in limiting billboards. The language of the bill specified that billboard owners must receive "just compensation" from the government when their signs were removed. Thus a large financial commitment from the government would be needed to achieve billboard control. In pursuing highway beautification, Lady Bird Johnson and the White House had passed an important marker in the legislative process, but the political price had been high. One White House aide said, "Some of our best friends are shaking their heads in disbelief that we have made ourselves look so inept." The Johnson administration was seeking a billboard-control bill that was stronger than Congress would accept, and the White House was making substantial concessions to get any bill through on Capitol Hill.[15]

The House Public Works Committee reported out its version of highway beautification on 21 September. The White House noted realistically that "there is not evident at this point any broad, enthusiastic support for the bill." By fall 1965, Congress was showing the strain of the session that had enacted Great Society legislation, and as Lyndon Johnson had foreseen, the large Democratic majorities that the 1964 election had produced were growing weary and restive.[16]

Further evidence of trouble for the White House occurred when the House Rules Committee sent the bill to the floor by a narrow 7 to

6 margin. For a bill "that the President — and Mrs. Johnson — want badly" the prospects were less than promising. Lady Bird Johnson decided to step up her public involvement in the legislative battle. In letters to probillboard advocates she wrote, "I know that the people of this country will be disappointed — as I will — if a bill on highway improvement is not enacted before Congress adjourns." She sent Liz Carpenter to the House to see lawmakers in person. Carpenter, in her own words, "put on my best Joy perfume and tightest girdle" and visited undecided Texas legislators. George H. Mahon (D-TX), an influential member, summarized the state of affairs in Congress for Carpenter: "No one in the Texas delegation likes the bill, but no one wants to vote against Lady Bird." [17]

As the voting neared, Mrs. Johnson tried to ease the fears of the antibillboard forces about the overall merits of the bill. She thought the legislation represented "reasonable regulation, and thus is a major stride toward achieving the goal of beauty along our highways to which we all aspire." During the first week of October, the White House concluded that it would be best to bring the bill up on Thursday, 7 October, "because the members want to go home and are tired of hearing about the bill." Faced with the prospect of an "ungallant rejection of Mrs. Johnson's special project," House leaders were "counting noses and twisting arms to beat the band on this one." [18]

As the voting neared, the situation became even more complicated. The president, suffering from an ailing gall bladder, planned to enter Bethesda Naval Hospital for surgery the next day. Before that difficulty had arisen, the Johnsons had scheduled a gala Salute to Congress, with entertainment by Fredric March, Anita Bryant, Gordon and Sheila MacRae, and the Ned Odum Boys, among others. Senate and House members were supposed to meet at the White House, have a drink, and then be bused to the State Department for the entertainment and celebration of the productive session. The schedule of the gala hinged on the House's concluding its business by late afternoon on Thursday.

The highway beautification bill, however, did not come up for debate until late in the evening. As talk ran into the night, the president's insistence on getting the bill passed for Mrs. Johnson's sake became key to the situation. House members heard that Johnson had told some Democrats that "he would rather have the bill for which his wife had campaigned zealously, than to go ahead with the Salute." Republicans complained that they would not be welcome at the festivities without the beautification bill. The Salute continued late into the evening, as senators, their wives, and the wives of congressmen listened to what proved to be rousing music and dramatic readings. As the evening ended, President Johnson said good night to his audience. He was sorry that the House members could not be there, but "they saw their duty and I hope they're doing it [applause] and I believe they are." [19]

On the House floor, "duty" came to symbolize Mrs. Johnson's role in highway beautification, and the Republicans vented their frustration toward both the Johnsons. One congressman called it "the president's wife's bill"; Melvin R. Laird (R-WI) complained about press reports that "we must pass this bill tonight so that it can delivered to the lovely First Lady as a present or package at the White House party." One young Republican, Robert Dole of Kansas, offered a semiplayful amendment to delete the phrase "Secretary of Commerce" wherever it appeared in the bill and to substitute "Lady Bird." The amendment failed on a voice vote. [20]

The bill itself finally passed late that night with some language that the White House did not want. Faced with the likelihood that any changes in the wording would cause the entire bill to collapse, the administration decided to accept what it could get. On 13 October the Senate concurred in the bill as the House had passed it, and the measure went to President Johnson for his signature.

The bill-signing ceremony took place in the East Room of the White House on 22 October 1965. "The atmosphere was pleasant and relaxed," wrote a Commerce official, and the president and his wife "mingled with us during the serving of coffee, punch, etc." "The law," said the president in his remarks, "will bring the wonders of nature back into our daily lives." Everyone in the room knew that the Highway Beautification Act was imperfect, but the Johnsons recognized that it was the only version the Congress would pass. Lady Bird Johnson did not speak at the ceremony, but photographs showed her pleased expression as her husband gave her one of the pens. In the letters that she sent out that autumn, she noted, "Isn't it wonderful that Congress has made highway beautification the law of the land?" [21]

Lady Bird Johnson, the president, and congressional leaders at the
signing of the Highway Beautification Act, 22 October 1965.
(LBJ Library, Yoichi R. Okamoto photograph)

The passage of the Highway Beautification Act increased Lady
Bird Johnson's visibility as an activist First Lady. "Lady Bird Wins on
Billboards," said an editorial in the *Washington Star,* and a cartoonist depicted her with a sword, jousting with a monster on a billboard,
under the caption "Beauty and the Beast." She had performed in "a
new 'First Lady' role" in securing the bill's passage, wrote the editors
of the *Christian Science Monitor.* That judgment was accurate: Lady
Bird Johnson had moved beyond the precedents of Ellen Wilson and
her alley legislation in 1914, Eleanor Roosevelt's public role in the
1940s, and Jacqueline Kennedy's advocacy of White House restoration to immerse herself in the details of environmental legislation.[22]

Public visibility, however, also meant political criticism. "This
legislation is a WHIM of Mrs. Johnson," the owner of the Dallas
Outdoor Advertising Company wrote the president, "and you are
backing it to the hilt to please her with no regard to the effect it will
have on thousands and thousands of people in the Outdoor Advertising Business." In Montana a billboard appeared briefly, calling
for "Impeachment of Lady Bird," which led cartoonist Bill Mauldin
to depict a landscape festooned with billboards, one of which read
"Impeach Lady Bird."[23]

For Congressman Dole, firing his public slingshot at the First

*Bill Mauldin, "Impeach Lady Bird." (Reprinted with special permission
from the Chicago Sun–Times, Inc., copyright 1999)*

Lady led to criticism from his Democratic colleagues on the House
floor. In the face of the attacks, Dole responded that Mrs. Johnson had taken an "active interest" in the legislation. He added that
"when one chooses to step down from the pedestal of the dutiful,
preoccupied wife of the president, or other public official, and to
wade into the turbulent stream of public controversy, one must expect to, at least, get her feet wet." Thirty years later, when Dole ran

for president, Bill Clinton's campaign used the episode as one early example of Dole's political nastiness.[24]

Lady Bird Johnson's reaction to these events, from Dole's comments to Mauldin's cartoon, was measured. "Imagine me keeping company with Chief Justice Warren!" she observed in response to the billboards that called for her impeachment. Her response to being an object of public controversy herself was more guarded. Her associates remembered that she decided to be more careful and less visible but no less active in her support of beautification measures involving highways. She knew that publicity was the most powerful weapon that a First Lady could exercise but that it had to be employed in ways that were unifying and nonpartisan. As Dole's comments indicated, there were limits in the 1960s to what a male-dominated society would accept from the wife of a president if she openly moved from being a celebrity to a leader of a substantive cause.[25]

What Lady Bird Johnson had achieved with the Highway Beautification Act represented a notable step forward in the historical role of the First Lady. She had shown that the wife of the president could be a player on Capitol Hill with the right cause and the right tactics. The participation of the wife of the president did not guarantee success, as Hillary Rodham Clinton learned in the 1990s in her health care campaign. But Lady Bird Johnson had stretched the limits of the possible for those First Ladies who followed her.

The law that she saw passed was neither strong nor effective in regulating billboards. The agreement to provide "just compensation" for billboard owners established a bad precedent. Other problems emerged as the law was interpreted and the billboard lobby sought to water it down even more. Although a better law might have been prepared had the Johnson White House galvanized conservation support in the 1960s, even that possibility was unlikely. At bottom, Congress had a pervasive lack of enthusiasm for any billboard control during the 1960s. Had the Highway Beautification Act not been passed in October 1965, there was no other time when it could have been enacted.

Part of the problem in 1965 for the White House and the First Lady was a lack of expertise in the workings of billboard control. Lyndon Johnson sought generalists on his staff, not experts. This approach made sense in dealing with the ever-changing array of

problems that came to the presidency. But when a complex, tech-
nical issue such as billboard control was involved, the intelligence
of Bill Moyers was no match for the inside knowledge of Phillip
Tocker. Nor did Lady Bird Johnson have a trained staff who could
delve into environmental issues directly.

The White House might have reached out to roadside councils
and other environmental groups for help but did not do so. One
difficulty was the lack of any environmental coalition as such in
1965. Roadside councils had no national organization and no way
to mobilize their members. These groups were composed largely of
women, and the White House and Congress shared the implicit assumption that whenever women were involved, common sense and
practicality were absent. Thus when the First Lady and her aides became involved in highway beautification, their presence evoked an
elaborate display of feigned courtesy that masked a high degree of
male condescension.

Nonetheless, in the process of getting even an imperfect bill
through, Lady Bird Johnson was a central catalyst. She supplied the
initial impetus to her husband in November and December 1964.
The momentum that she imparted sustained the campaign through
the White House Conference on Natural Beauty and into summer
1965. When Congress began committee consideration, her interven-
tion kept the bill alive in the House. She supplied overall direction
to the lobbying campaign once the measure reached the floor of
Congress. Without her commitment the bill would not have been
passed. Lyndon Johnson also deserves much credit for his strong
support of the bill, but it was his wife who had channeled his energies in the way that she desired.

Like the president, Lady Bird Johnson deemed the Highway
Beautification Act a promising start. The future of the bill hinged on
the way that the law was administered in its formative years. Though
she did so with less public visibility, Mrs. Johnson displayed as much
leadership in working on the implementation of the act as she had
put forth in sponsoring the law originally. In fact, her involvement
with Congress in this phase of the struggle was even more extensive
than it had been during the passage of the bill itself.

During the two years after the passage of the act, the outdoor advertising industry endeavored to water down the statute. The OAAA
mobilized its allies in Congress to limit the power of the Secretary of

Commerce to write regulations under the new act. As for the regulations themselves, the association tried to see that the size and spacing of billboards under these rules gave the industry as much leeway as possible. The First Lady and her staff followed closely the process by which the Commerce Department wrote and implemented regulations to enforce the law. That involvement required Mrs. Johnson's staff to become enmeshed in the details of billboard regulation. Throughout 1966 Mrs. Johnson discovered that congressional support for a strong regulatory policy toward outdoor advertising was eroding. Lawmakers removed funding for billboard control from the 1966 federal highway act. "This is a program," said one Republican lawmaker, "that could well be held in abeyance while the administration attempts to get its fiscal house in order." [26]

Nonetheless, Mrs. Johnson remained committed to the antibillboard campaign in 1967. She sought stronger enforcement through the appointment of a coordinator of highway beautification in the Bureau of Public Roads who agreed with her goals. That effort succeeded with the naming of California state senator Fred Farr to the post that same year. The First Lady found herself caught between mounting congressional opposition as the Vietnam War drained away funds for social projects and the conservation forces who wanted an even tougher law on the books. To galvanize the pro-beauty forces, Mrs. Johnson and her staff wrote speeches for representatives and had these documents inserted in the *Congressional Record.* [27]

Throughout these years, Lady Bird Johnson and the people around her had to respond to charges that she and her husband wanted highway beautification for selfish reasons. Rumors circulated that the Johnsons wanted to restrict outdoor advertising because of their television holdings. In early 1966 the White House received a report that in Minnesota, Arizona, and North Dakota, there were claims that "the reason the Johnsons want to do away with highway signs is that they have television interests and that way, TV will get all the advertising. Hence the campaign by Lady Bird Johnson to beautify the highways to cut down on advertising signs." Though Mrs. Johnson was probably aware of how billboard advertising related to their media holdings in a general way, she did not base her views on the effects of outdoor advertising on her personal financial interests or television station holdings. As for her husband, if he was for billboard regulation because she wanted it, it is hard to see how he could also have harbored a hidden financial agenda at the same time.[28]

As 1967 progressed, it became apparent that the White House and the First Lady would be hard-pressed to keep the Highway Beautification Act in existence. A stronger version was politically impossible. Within the federal government, other agencies used billboards for advertising in a manner that sabotaged Mrs. Johnson's efforts. "Until the Federal agencies set an example," lamented Liz Carpenter in 1967, "the administration is going to be subject to valid criticism of not practicing what we preach." [29]

The goal of the Johnson administration in 1967 was to remove funding for billboard regulation from close congressional scrutiny. The White House wanted to see a trust fund established that would pay billboard operators for taking down their signs. Congress rejected the idea but did provide some appropriations for enforcement of the law. Clearly, the tide was running against this reform in Congress. Columnist Drew Pearson told his readers that "a skillful lobbying drive against Lady Bird Johnson's beautification program appears to be bearing fruit." After surveying prospects on Capitol Hill, one of Lyndon Johnson's operatives told the president, "We are so far away from having a majority that considering the economy mood of the House and the increasing pressure for adjournment we would lose the bill on the floor." The First Lady decided, after consulting with her husband, that the best strategy would be to make another effort to secure funding in 1968.[30]

The situation remained unchanged in 1968, however. The trust fund idea stalled in a House committee, and the legislative leadership sliced the appropriation for billboard regulation to $8.5 million. Despite this setback, Lady Bird Johnson lobbied as hard in 1968 as she had in 1965 for positive congressional action to keep billboard control alive as a policy. Once the bill was passed, she agreed with her husband that he had to sign the measure despite its flaws. If the president had vetoed it, highway beautification might well have been dropped altogether. The Federal-Aid Highway Act of 1968 delivered a serious blow to the antibillboard forces, but there was virtually nothing that the White House could do but to accept the meager results of what once had been an ambitious program.[31]

Another aspect of highway policy that Lady Bird Johnson became involved in during her fight against billboards had to do with the location of new road construction. In 1965, for example, Sharon Francis reported that the First Lady was receiving letters "from citizens who are disturbed and shocked by proposed route locations that are destroying irreplaceable parks and spots of natural beauty." Although the First Lady could have little substantive impact on the power of the highway construction issue, she did tell the American Road Builders at their convention in February 1966 that "we must also weigh in the social and esthetic values of the routing" of highways. She then added, "What a tragedy it will be if we do not make our highways instruments of beauty as well as convenience in the vast construction program which lies ahead of us." [32]

The highway-location issue continued to elicit large amounts of mail over the next several years. Residents of New Orleans, San Antonio, and numerous other cities where freeways were being built wrote to seek her assistance. She prodded the Bureau of Public Roads to a greater awareness of the issue by supporting congressional efforts to have parks and historic sites spared in interstate highway construction. It was never easy. As Sharon Francis wrote in early 1967, "Changing the course of history—or of a bureaucracy is something akin to nudging a steamship in mid-ocean." Flying over the New Jersey highway system later that year, the First Lady commented, "Freeways are efficient, they get you where you are going in a hurry. But we are just now beginning to do something about the esthetic values of highways." In this area, Lady Bird Johnson could only set an example for policymakers and serve as a rallying point for citizens concerned about proliferating highways.[33]

With the passage of the 1968 highway law, Mrs. Johnson's active involvement as First Lady with highway beautification and billboard control came to an end. In the years after 1969, the Highway Beautification Act was often criticized as an ineffective piece of legislation that actually promoted the interests of billboard owners. To the degree that that was in fact the case, it was not Lady Bird Johnson's fault. The law that she helped enact in 1965 was as vigorous a measure as the political forces in Congress would allow. Indeed she was the political catalyst that gave billboard regulation a chance to survive throughout the 1960s.

In the years after Mrs. Johnson left the White House, her popular

identification with the act persisted, and her involvement with roadside issues grew. In 1969 she decided to sponsor an annual series of
beautification awards to be given to members of the Texas Highway
Department. Presented each fall at the LBJ State Park in Stonewall,
the awards recognized the use of wildflowers, roadside parks, and
the maintenance of roadside plants and shrubs that were installed
as part of the scenic enhancement under the 1965 law. Looking back
on the awards program in 1980, she hoped that it had "helped to
make preservation and propagation of our natural assets an on-
going aim — happening naturally in the course of a day's work." The
spirit of these occasions — relaxed, informal, and good-humored —
suggested that she had accomplished much of her aim in establishing the awards.[34]

The law that she had sponsored in 1965 remained a significant
source of controversy among environmentalists during the 1970s
and 1980s. Some progress did occur in landscaping and scenic improvement. By 1979 the Department of Transportation reported that
2,300 junkyards had been removed or screened and another 1,055
illegal ones had been removed. There were, however, almost 11,000
illegal junkyards that still required government action.[35]

On billboard control, the positions of the industry and the environmentalists had reversed themselves since the 1960s. The outdoor
advertising industry had become staunch defenders of the Highway Beautification Act while proponents of regulation labeled it as
probusiness and ineffective. Some individuals in the antibillboard
coalition even wanted the act repealed. There was little chance that
there would ever be enough government money to compensate all
the billboard owners for taking their signs down. Meanwhile, the
existing federal legislation stood in the way of local and state efforts
to control highway clutter.

Lady Bird Johnson remained an active proponent of billboard
regulation in the 1970s and 1980s. When budget restrictions produced a cutback in funding for the billboard removal program during the Carter and Reagan years, she expressed her concerns. "Of
course I regret the omission of highway beautification funds from
the budget," she said in 1979, "but I do understand the urgency of
curtailing all possible spending in order to hold down inflation." In
the mid-1980s, proponents of control made a major effort in Con-

gress to remove the "just-compensation" provision from the 1965 law that had been such a barrier to progress. Lady Bird Johnson and Laurance Rockefeller sent a joint telegram in September 1986 supporting that approach: "We encourage your support of this reform, which is needed to restore the scenic beauty of our nation's highways." When the amendment came to the floor of the Senate on 3 February 1987, the president of the OAAA was watching from the members' gallery; his organization had contributed $350,000 in campaign funds and honoraria to members of Congress between 1983 and 1985. The amendment was soundly defeated by a vote of 57 to 40. The alignment of probillboard forces that Lady Bird Johnson had confronted in the 1960s remained intact and powerful.[36]

The Highway Beautification Act is still known as Lady Bird Johnson's law, even though it has disappointed its friends and encouraged its enemies. Yet there was never a choice between the law as it was passed in October 1965 and a more perfect measure. The dilemma for the advocates of beautification was to choose between no regulation at all or the halfway step of the 1965 bill.

From 1966 to 20 January 1969, Lady Bird Johnson sustained the highway beautification program with her personal commitment and influence. No one in the government who was in a position of authority cared about it as much as she did, and no one with power gave it as much backing as she gave it. Her efforts, coupled with her influence on her husband, prevented the program from disappearing in a Congress that was angry over the Vietnam War and was determined to cut back on social programs. Lady Bird Johnson was the essential element that kept highway beautification alive as an administration program during the 1960s.

Had she done nothing about highway beautification as First Lady, the effort would probably have sputtered along in the rear of environmental issues. Instead, the act made the problem a matter of continuing national debate. President Bill Clinton recognized Mrs. Johnson's historic contribution as an activist First Lady when he said in August 1997, "The effort she launched a generation ago to beautify our highways has reaped benefits in all fifty states and helped to inspire our nation's commitment to environmental protection."[37]

CHAPTER 6

HER SPACE
IN THE WORLD

Lady Bird Johnson's contributions as First Lady extended beyond the beautification of Washington, DC and the fight for billboard control. Her skill at preaching the gospel of beautification to audiences, the highly visible tours that she took to wilderness or threatened areas, and her role as an environmental advocate within the federal government laid the basis for the contributions she made to American life through the end of the twentieth century.

Although Mrs. Johnson had established herself as a leading exponent of the environment within the Johnson presidency, maintaining that position was often a more formidable task than it appeared to be. She faced the institutional obstacles that confront all First Ladies. She first had to persuade the White House staff that she was a legitimate player in the administration. Lacking a First Lady's office, as her successors would have, she had to borrow people from the Interior Department and other agencies. This approach brought her talented individuals such as Sharon Francis and Cynthia Wilson, but it also meant that she had to finance much of her work from her own pocket or ask her staff members to bear the burdens personally. Lady Bird Johnson did much to institutionalize the role of the president's wife in the government, but she had to do it through improvisation and from a skimpy financial base.

The traditional techniques of speeches and tours offered one effective means of getting her message out. Sharon Francis and Liz Carpenter wrote many of the First Lady's remarks, but she played an active part in the drafting of important addresses. She reached out to reporters and others for ideas, and she remembered to sound consistent themes to all her audiences. "Beauty cannot be set aside for vacations or special occasions," she told the National Council of State Garden Clubs and the American Forestry Association in September 1965. "It cannot be the occasional privilege of those who came long distances to visit nature. It cannot be reserved 'for nice neighborhoods ONLY.'" She was an instinctive consensus builder and sought to draw groups together to achieve joint action, often without relying on the federal government for support.[1]

A key to her success was her adroit use of tours to dramatize environmental issues. She knew that the media would follow her rafting adventures and her visits to redwood forests. The newswomen who covered her, said Liz Carpenter, "want an activist First Lady" because of the professional advancement it offered to these journalists. Though both sides knew that they were using each other, a genuine rapport developed between the First Lady and the reporters. She flew in the same plane with the journalists, and they shared the same food and accommodations. At the end of the presidency, the newspaperwomen offered her an affectionate parody: "Thanks for the memories / Of Big Bend rattlesnakes / Of barbecues and steaks / Of conservation / Restoration / And New England lobster bakes. . . . We thank you so much."[2]

A visit to the Big Bend in Texas in spring 1966 became one of the most celebrated of the First lady's excursions during her White House years. On 2 April a party that included Mrs. Johnson, Stewart Udall, Liz Carpenter, and about 100 others hiked through the park, camped on a mesa, and prepared for a journey down the Rio Grande.

The next day twenty-four rafts, with five or six people in each, took an eleven-mile ride down the river. One female reporter wore "a black and white polka-dot bikini, with a figure to suit it." At the conclusion of the turbulent ride, an exhausted Liz Carpenter observed that she liked most "the parks where all the concessions are run by the Rockefellers." The publicity caused tourist attendance at the park to rise during the ensuing weeks.[3]

Lady Bird Johnson and Stewart Udall, 2 April 1966, in the Big Bend Park.
(LBJ Library, Robert Knudsen photograph, C1616-17A)

As the presidency progressed and the Vietnam War wore on, however, the First Lady's speaking appearances became more controversial. When she visited Williams College and Yale University to deliver addresses on the environment, she encountered antiwar protestors. At Williams, part of the graduating class walked out, but the remaining audience then gave her a standing ovation. Her speech was well received, though she concluded that going to Williams was "probably a mistake on balance" because it provided the demonstrators with the opportunity "to get inches in the paper and on the television screen that they would not have gotten without me." That night she had a phone call from the president, who said, "I just hate for you to have to take that sort of thing." [4]

The next day at Yale there were 1,200 students standing in silent protest outside the hall where she was to appear. Inside, the members of the Yale Political Union received her warmly, and she spoke to "a very quiet, attentive audience." Although her speech was again successful, when she returned to Washington she seemed to Sharon Francis "very disheartened and upset." Perhaps, the First Lady observed, "she just shouldn't go on campuses any more." But by the time she prepared her diary entry a few days later, she had decided, "I must not live only in the White House, insulated against life. I want to know what's going on — even if to know is to suffer." [5]

Two areas in which Lady Bird Johnson tried to extend the reach of her beautification campaign included the business community and the federal government itself. In both cases, her celebrity and commitment produced some results but ultimately were disappointing. She was energetic in approaching corporations for support almost from the outset of her endeavor. She tried to persuade Texaco to carry forward a Service Station Beautification Program. Despite public assurances, very little occurred to change the look of service stations across the country. [6]

Some businesses provided moderate support. The Reliance Insurance Company planted trees near low-income schools in Philadelphia. The grocery chain Giant Food in Washington did some upgrading of parking lots and shopping centers, involved employees with the local community, and appointed at least one African American as manager. When the riots erupted in Washington in April 1968, the Giant outlets "were spared destruction, although they were located in the midst of the devastated area." Despite these occasional accomplishments, business proved unreceptive to Mrs. Johnson's efforts. Laurance Rockefeller was the only notable exception. [7]

Within the federal government itself, Lady Bird Johnson did not confront an overt sluggishness about the merits of beautification; few bureaucrats or agencies wanted to be in direct opposition to the president's wife. Instead, she had to struggle against the perception that even though her goals were worthwhile in an abstract sense, they should not outweigh the more practical and realistic needs of busy men in the White House or the executive branch. Nonetheless, the First Lady wielded her influence to promote public occasions where the federal government could stress beautification, to strengthen those agencies that protected the environment, and to advance candidates for government positions who shared her views on conservation questions.

Sponsoring conferences modeled on the White House Conference on Natural Beauty was one strategy that she followed. She endorsed state conferences on the environmental crisis, the most notably successful one in her native Texas in November 1965. She devoted a great deal of time and energy to the National Youth Conference on Natural Beauty and Conservation in summer 1966. Her niece, Diana MacArthur, served as a principal organizer for the gathering. After the meeting occurred, she encouraged what became a presidential announcement of a Youth Natural Beauty and Conservation Year in late 1967. The programs that emerged from the conference and the declaration extended the reach of Lady Bird Johnson's program among young people.[8]

Within the federal government, the First Lady paid close attention to those agencies that could promote the cause of the environment. She and her staff followed closely the work of the President's Council on Recreation and Natural Beauty and the Citizens' Advisory Committee on Recreation and Natural Beauty as they dealt with issues relating to scenic roads and billboards. She lobbied Congress to retain funding for these two groups, and she participated when appointments were made to see that individuals sympathetic to natural beauty were selected. She did what she could to ensure that eligible women were among the people considered for these posts.

As environmental controversies flared during the Johnson administration, interested groups sought to obtain the First Lady's endorsement of their position. Most of the time her staff deflected these initiatives to the government agency responsible for the policy decision. In the case of the Grand Canyon and the California redwoods, however, Mrs. Johnson had to express herself. These episodes underscored how much the public had come to regard her as a voice within the White House that spoke for the environment.

During the mid-1960s the Bureau of Reclamation in the Department of the Interior proposed to construct two dams in the Grand

Canyon to bring more water to the Arizona desert. The Sierra Club and other conservationists fought to block the dams and preserve the Canyon in its unspoiled state. Instead of simply referring the protest mail that poured into her office to Interior, Mrs. Johnson instructed her staff to answer the mail themselves. She believed that "she could not afford to preach natural beauty and ignore what was happening to the greatest beauty of them all—Grand Canyon." Some of her correspondence became public, and the extent to which she made protest legitimate underscored her role in supporting the movement to preserve the Grand Canyon.[9]

In the case of the California redwoods and the proposed national park, the First Lady's role was in advocating that the administration do its best to preserve as many of the ancient trees as possible. She sent Sharon Francis to California to make a report in 1967, and she let others in the administration know about how she felt. The First Lady's support was on the margins of the controversy, but she did have a constructive role in what became the Redwoods National Park Law in October 1968. It was appropriate that she was present on 27 August 1969, when the Lady Bird Johnson Grove was dedicated in the new Redwood National Park.

Throughout the months and years of her work for the environment in the White House, Lady Bird Johnson relied on the consistent and enthusiastic support of her husband. In his public statements, Lyndon Johnson underscored that he believed in what she was doing. In 1966, when the President's Council on Recreation and Natural Beauty was established, the president observed wryly that "for all my personal interest in beautification, some people, including some very close to me and on the platform this morning, seem to think that I am not quite interested enough. Sometimes she has to prod me a little bit. Sometimes I would actually swear that she is shoving." There were times when the president would lapse into a jocular tone about his wife's interest. Using a slight edge of sarcasm in public references to a spouse was, for men of his region, preferable to an outright declaration of love and respect, which might seem too sentimental and less manly. For Lyndon Johnson, this kind of presidential teasing was his way of saying that he admired and respected the First Lady's efforts.[10]

The partnership that the Johnsons had forged received its most severe test during the troubled months of late 1967 and early 1968 when the question of Lyndon's running again in 1968 became a central topic of concern. For the First Lady, the overriding issue was her husband's health. Ever since the heart attack in 1955 she had feared that another illness would leave him debilitated. The memory of Woodrow Wilson's stroke and infirmity from 1919 to 1921 was much on her mind. When the president had gall bladder problems in 1965, her thoughts went back to the heart attack: "For a long time — months, years — I have been keenly aware of how lucky we have been."[11]

The First Lady wrote in her diary in May 1967 about her feelings toward a second administration: "I do not know whether we can endure another four-year term in the presidency." She regarded the prospect "like an open-ended stay in a concentration camp." In her view, the president should emulate Harry Truman's action in 1952 and announce his withdrawal from the race in March 1968.[12]

By summer 1967 the Johnsons jointly had decided that he would not run again. The question then became the exact timing of the announcement. Throughout the fall, prospective dates came and went. In early January the presidential couple talked with their friends John and Nellie Connally about when to make the public statement. Connally himself had already announced himself that he would not run again for governor of Texas in 1968. After much conversation, their talks ended indecisively. "Who knows, who knows," wrote the First Lady, "and so we went round and round on the same hot griddle, finding no cool oasis, no definite time for an acceptable exit."[13]

For a moment it seemed as if the president might act on 17 January at the end of his State of the Union message. During the cold afternoon, Lady Bird Johnson went with Sharon Francis, Laurance Rockefeller, and New York philanthropist Brooke Astor to visit the Buchanan School in Washington. Later the First Lady had a moment with her husband. "Well, what do you think?" he asked, "what shall I do?" She answered that their daughters were divided; as for herself, she said, "Me — I don't know. I have said it all before. I can't tell you what to do." Once again, Lyndon Johnson stalled, and the announcement did not occur.[14]

The next day, Lady Bird Johnson encountered the most trying

personal moment of her years as First Lady. She had scheduled the first Women Doers luncheon of 1968 on the general topic of crime in the streets. The event brought together some fifty women who were active in anticrime areas. One of the guests was the black actress and singer Eartha Kitt, who had been recommended to Liz Carpenter and Sharon Francis as someone who had testified on behalf of the administration's anticrime bill. Kitt's career had trailed off somewhat since her theatrical debut in the early 1950s and a series of hit records. Yet no one had any reason to predict that she would make a personal protest.

After the First Lady made her prepared remarks, several women spoke to the group about what they had done to curb crime. Midway through the meeting, Lyndon Johnson came in. As he left, he and Kitt exchanged comments about crime, day care, and Social Security. Alert to Kitt's mood, Mrs. Johnson watched as "she smoldered and smoked." [15] When the question period began, Kitt was recognized, and she started with remarks that lasted for about five minutes. "We send the best of this country off to be shot and maimed. They rebel in the streets. They take pot and they will get high. They don't want to go to school, because they are going to be snatched from their mothers to be shot in Vietnam." [16]

Lady Bird Johnson kept her eyes on Eartha Kitt, matching her "stare for stare." The singer repeated herself several times and then concluded. "You are a mother, too, although you have had daughters and not sons. I am a mother and I know the feeling of having a baby come out of my guts. I have a baby and then you send him off to war. No wonder the kids rebel and take pot. And, Mrs. Johnson, in case you don't understand the lingo, that's marijuana!" [17]

As she heard Kitt's impassioned remarks, the First Lady experienced what she remembered as a "surge of adrenalin into the blood, knowing that you are going to answer, that you've *got* to answer, that you *want* to answer, and at the same time somewhere in the back of your mind a voice that says, 'Be calm, be dignified.' " In a trembling voice, but without the tears that the press reported, she said, "Because there is a war on—and I pray that there will be a just and honest peace—that doesn't give us a free ticket not to try to work for better things—against crime in the streets, and for better education and better health for our people." Eartha Kitt remembered that Mrs. Johnson said only, "Miss Kitt, just because there's a war on doesn't mean we can't be civilized." The First Lady's diary indicates that she concluded by saying, "I cannot identify as much as I should. I have not lived the background that you have, nor can I speak as passionately or as well, but we must keep our eyes and our hearts and our energies fixed on constructive areas and try to do something that will make this a happier, better-educated land."[18]

The room filled with applause as Mrs. Johnson finished. By late afternoon the episode with Kitt was on the national news services. The singer told *Newsweek* that "if Mrs. Johnson was embarrassed, that's her problem." Kitt's career declined over the next ten years because, as she believed, of governmental probes into her actions. President Johnson was sent a file that the CIA had assembled about her in the 1950s, but there was no official response to the incident. The White House received some 35,000 letters about an instance that revealed the degree to which Vietnam had polarized the nation by winter 1968.[19]

The next two-and-a-half months were filled with dramatic events. The Tet offensive and the political challenges to Lyndon Johnson from Eugene J. McCarthy and Robert F. Kennedy raised doubts about the president's ability to win renomination. In her diary Lady Bird Johnson focused on the uncertain state of her husband's health. By 31 March 1968, they had come to the brink of making the withdrawal statement.

The speech including the surprise announcement was made at 9:00 P.M. "Remember—pacing and drama," she told her husband just before he began, with the kind of gentle coaching she had been doing for years. She knew that her husband did not come across well on television, that he was "never really comfortable" with the medium. But that night it worked. The moments afterward were for her "a great blur of confusion," and then she met with friends on the second floor: "Nearly everyone just looked staggered and struck silent—and then the phones began to ring." Later, for the clamoring reporters, Lady Bird Johnson issued her own statement: "We have done a lot; there's a lot left to do in the remaining months; maybe this is the only way to get it done."[20]

During the final ten months of her husband's presidency, she continued the pattern she had already established as First Lady. She

Lady Bird Johnson amid the California redwoods, 25 November 1968.
(LBJ Library, Robert Knudsen photograph, D2624-7A)

made trips to Texas, Connecticut, and Arizona. She also gave the
B. Y. Morrison Memorial Lecture to the annual convention of the
American Institute of Architects. She spoke about a "new conservation" in architecture that had "a concern for the total environment — not just the individual building, but the entire community."

At the end she stated her basic creed: "The nature we are concerned with, ultimately, is *human* nature. That is the point of the beautification movement — and that, finally, is the point of architecture."[21]

One legislative achievement of the final months gave her lasting pleasure. On 15 July the president signed a law that amended the Land and Water Conservation Fund, which had been created in 1964. The fund would receive revenues from mineral leases from drilling on the outer continental shelf, a change that raised the fund's annual income to $200 million. Wilderness and park acquisitions would be paid for from these funds. Lady Bird Johnson said sixteen years later that this "little-known" change in the funding for the wilderness was one of the reasons that she and her husband deserved credit for launching the environmental movement during the 1960s.[22]

As the end of the presidency approached, the First Lady and her aides looked for ways to establish her legacy on a more permanent basis. She did not wish "to try to bind the next First Lady" in whatever she did. However, she did hope that the committee she had created might have some enduring framework. In this attempt, however, Mrs. Johnson ran up against the inherent limitations of her position. The possibility of an executive order establishing the committee was discussed, but the White House staff reported that "the First Lady has never been given official duties by law or executive order, and this would be a break with tradition."[23]

Since the woman who came after Lady Bird Johnson would determine for herself what she would do as the wife of the president, a consensus emerged that nothing should be done. In a memo to the First Lady, Joseph Califano, one of Lyndon Johnson's senior aides, concluded that neither an executive order nor making the committee responsible to Mayor Walter Washington would be appropriate. Mrs. Johnson's unwillingness to impose the crusade for beautification on the next First Lady remained consistent during her last days in the White House.[24]

She looked forward to the final meetings of her committee in fall 1968, yet her mind was on many issues as the meeting of 2 October neared. The long struggle to confirm Abe Fortas as chief justice was ending in failure. Mrs. Johnson had suggested that her husband nominate a woman to the Supreme Court, but that had not come to pass. The Johnsons did take pride in the four conservation measures signed into law on that day, the most important of which established the Redwoods Park in California. In his signing statement, President Johnson called his wife an "enthusiastic, tenacious, pugnacious, persistent advocate of conservation every hour in this house." Then she had a warm and rewarding meeting with her committee.[25]

The month that followed was eventful. Jacqueline Kennedy married Aristotle Onassis, an occasion that left Lady Bird Johnson "strangely freer. No shadow walks beside me down the halls of the White House or here at Camp David." A few days later, her daughter Lynda had her first child. Then Richard Nixon defeated Hubert Humphrey in the presidential election.[26]

It was snowing in Washington on 12 November when the First Lady's committee gathered in the Department of the Interior's auditorium. There were gifts: from the Inaugural Committee, 220 dogwood trees; from the Society for a More Beautiful National Capital, 1 million daffodils, thanks to the generosity of Mary Lasker, and from the society and the Park Service, 2,500 dogwoods; and more than a mile of trails through the city. After Mrs. Johnson had spoken, Stewart Udall made the special announcement that Columbia Island in the Potomac River was being renamed Lady Bird Johnson Park. "I was stunned," the First Lady recalled, "but, it can't be denied, pleased that they would want to do this for me." [27]

The approaching end of her tenure as First Lady evoked a series of retrospective assessments of her time in Washington. Shana Alexander, after accompanying Mrs. Johnson on a late November trip to the redwoods, "began to sense how much more Mrs. Johnson leaves behind her than daffodils coast to coast. Quite possibly she is the best First Lady we have ever had." The editors of *Christian Century* reached a similar conclusion: they credited Lady Bird Johnson with being "an inspirer of many movements to save our natural environment." [28]

For the First Lady herself, the end of her years in Washington produced understandably mixed emotions. Bess Abell recalled driving "out of the north portico" on "one of those crystal sky evenings. It just looked so beautiful and the lights were on in the White House and the lights were beginning to sparkle on the buildings there on Pennsylvania Avenue." As they moved "towards the northwest gate," Abell asked, "Oh, Mrs. Johnson, are you going to miss this?" The First Lady turned around and said, "Oh, yes, I'll miss it every day. I'll miss it like a front tooth. But you know there is absolutely nothing, absolutely nothing in the world that would make me willing to pay the price for another ticket of admission." [29]

The last weeks passed quickly. The committee met a final time on 17 December 1968. After all the speeches and festivities, Lyndon Johnson came in and thanked the members "for returning my wife to me" and told them that they "brought out the best in people." Nash Castro felt as the meeting ended "that this great First Lady had earned many pages in the history of the great American drama." [30]

Inauguration Day was hectic and emotional, but finally the former president and his wife were back in Texas, home again. Lady Bird Johnson went to bed after 9:00 P.M. and in her last entry in the diary that she had kept so long and so fully, her thoughts were of a poem: "I seek, to celebrate my glad release, the Tents of Silence and the Camp of Peace." As she conceded, it was not precisely "the right exit line for me because I have loved almost every day of these five years." [31]

What First Ladies do after their years in the White House varies as widely as the women themselves. In the twentieth century, the president's wife who lived the longest after leaving the White House was Edith Wilson, from 1921 to 1961. In her seventeen years from her husband's death in 1945 until she died in 1962, Eleanor Roosevelt served as an ambassador at the United Nations and then as an activist within the Democratic party. Jacqueline Kennedy Onassis remained an international celebrity and figure in American publishing until her death in 1994. Lady Bird Johnson has enjoyed three full decades since she and her husband left Washington, making her time as a former First Lady the third longest in this century.

Mrs. Johnson has been notable for the continuity of her interest in conservation and the environment, which has marked the years since the presidency. In that sense, she has set another precedent of consistency in following through on policy initiatives that her successors such as Betty Ford and Rosalynn Carter have emulated in Mrs. Ford's emphasis on treatment of alcoholism and in Mrs. Carter's on mental health.

Even before leaving Washington, Lady Bird Johnson had planned to carry on her beautification work on a smaller scale in Texas. "I will continue to be just as interested" in conservation, she said to Washington reporters, and "I think it is quite possible that in my smaller sphere I will at the same time be of some use to conservation." The extent of her involvement was most measured during the years before her husband died but expanded significantly during the late 1970s and into the 1980s.[32]

The most lasting commitment that Mrs. Johnson made during the first phase of the postpresidential years was the annual award ceremony, held at the LBJ Ranch, to honor the highway beautification programs of the Texas Highway Department. The ceremonies included a barbecue luncheon in addition to the awards themselves. Lyndon Johnson came to the first three occasions, in part, as he said in fun, to see his frugal wife give away money.[33]

In the introduction to *Texas: A Roadside View* (1980), Lady Bird Johnson surveyed the effects of her awards. She was pleased at "the protection of the fall flowers" and at the "planning, imagination, and commonsense the nominees have put to use"; she also hoped that the recognition of the highway officials would encourage in others "a growing sense of the importance of projects that save and use plant material so that we might realize the ecological benefits as well as enjoy the aesthetic results."[34]

In Austin during the early 1970s, Lady Bird Johnson became identified with the Town Lake Beautification Project along the Colorado River. "My interest in conservation-beautification continues unabating," she wrote Stewart Udall in April 1972, "though now on a very little stage—my current project is the Riverfront in Austin's hike and bike trail, *many* blooming trees (redbud, crepe myrtle, etc.)." She told an interviewer in 1980 that "we spent a busy five years raising funds," and the handsome parks and extensive running trails through the heart of the city, which were filled with joggers every day, reflected what she had accomplished for Austin. When Austinites tried to have the portion of the Colorado River known as Town Lake renamed for her, however, she always declined the honor. She said in 1974, "Each time I walk along the shores of the river, I come away feeling deeply satisfied in seeing our dreams becoming a reality, and Austin a more pleasant place in which to live and visit."[35]

One of the most gratifying aspects of the years from 1969 to 1973 was having her husband home with her. For the first time in their years together, Lyndon Johnson did not have to deal with immediate crises or answer the calls of public office. With the self-discipline of power behind him, he disregarded the strict regimen that he had observed since his 1955 heart attack. He ate what he wanted and resumed smoking. And he found time for the winter vacations in Mexico where they stayed in "a lovely sprawling hacienda with a breath-taking view of a mountain-ringed bay, vermilion sunsets, and tropical jungle foliage." When Johnson imposed on his staff or became excessively demanding, his wife would pause and say, as she had done so often, "My dear, just look on it all as one great adventure." [36]

Her husband made sure that she found time for the opportunities that came open for her during his retirement years. Late in 1970 the governor of Texas, Preston Smith, asked her to serve on the Board of Regents of the University of Texas system. She declined because of the uncertain state of Lyndon's health and her need to be at home. After she put down the telephone, Lyndon, who was listening to her from his bed, said, "Come in here, I think I know what you were talking about, but tell me." [37]

Once she had explained Smith's offer, Lyndon replied, "How did you feel when I would try to convince some really capable citizen to take a government job, a cabinet post, or head an agency, anything in the service of his country, and he said no because his family didn't want to move to Washington or because he was climbing the ladder in his company?" Lady Bird Johnson had always resented such behavior when she was in Washington because she wanted her husband "to get the best people." So she called Governor Smith and agreed to serve. [38]

Lyndon Johnson died on 22 January 1973 of a heart attack. Through her grief, she also told friends, "Wouldn't I be ungracious not to be terribly grateful for thirty-eight wonderful years?" Through the 1970s she pursued her own interests and traveled the world as she had not been able to do with her husband. She served her term as a regent at the University of Texas, managed the family's extensive business interests, and spent time with the growing families of her daughters. She quietly supported Democratic candidates with financial contributions, and she spoke out when the national highway beautification program was attacked. Partly because of the influence of her daughter Lynda Robb and her service on the President's Commission on Women, Lady Bird Johnson's own sense of commitment to feminist causes grew.[39]

As she approached her seventieth birthday in 1982, she chose a new project that reflected her lifelong interest in wildflowers and beautification. She noticed that the world around her in Austin was changing. "The open fields and meadows had disappeared and in their place were shopping malls, suburbs chock-a-block with housing developments and industrial plans and spaghetti networks of highways." She lamented that "gone were the scenes I loved along with much of the habitat for wildflowers and native plants." She resolved to do something "to keep alive the beauty I had known."[40]

The answer was the National Wildflower Research Center, which was begun with her donation of $125,000 and sixty acres of land east of Austin on 22 December 1982. It was her way, she told reporters, of "paying rent for the space I have taken up in this highly interesting world." Matching gifts from Laurance Rockefeller and others brought the initial endowment to $700,000 and enabled the center to begin its work in 1983.[41]

To help create the Wildflower Center, Lady Bird Johnson turned again to the techniques of fund-raising and publicity that she had used so effectively in the White House. Her old friend, Helen Hayes, the First Lady of the American Theater, became cochair with Mrs. Johnson as well as a member of the center's foundation. Drawing on the experience of her Committee to Beautify the Nation's Capital, Lady Bird Johnson reached out to other donors and associates from her days in the White House, including Rockefeller, Nash Castro, Mary Lasker, and Brooke Astor. A gala dinner in May 1985 in New York City where 600 guests paid up to $1,000 each helped launch the center in sparkling style. Mrs. Johnson had mastered the subtle art of linking philanthropy and the environment.

During its first thirteen years of operation, the Wildflower Center, under its first director David Northington, conducted research into the uses and effects of wildflowers in its 300,000 feet of space. In cooperation with highway departments in other states, it examined how the use of roadside flowers might reduce mowing and maintenance costs. Information poured in from around the nation.

Lady Bird Johnson at her Austin home, surrounded by bluebonnets, 1990s.
(author's collection, National Wildflower Research Center photograph)

Senator Lloyd Bentsen of Texas, another old friend of Mrs. Johnson, secured legislation to set aside federal highway funds for projects that encouraged the use of wildflowers. With Mrs. Johnson's name behind it and success in its research projects, the center's reach expanded. By the end of the 1980s, its membership had grown to more than 7,500. "My goal," Mrs. Johnson told a reporter, in December 1987, "is to get 10,000." [42]

As the center grew larger in the early 1990s, it became evident that the original site on the eastern edge of Austin was becoming inadequate. The area lacked the variety of plants more characteristic of the Hill Country, which began on the western side of the city. "We are at a stage where we cannot continue to grow and to provide the public education needed without expanding our physical facilities and staff," Northington said in June 1991. [43]

Mrs. Johnson acquired property for the center in the Circle C developments southwest of Austin, and plans for relocation proceeded. The development was controversial in local politics, as the issue of urban growth and sprawl shaped many city elections. Mrs. Johnson's decision to work with a project that suggested such problems caused some unfavorable reaction in the Austin environmental community. For her the choice represented the kind of constructive partnership with the business community that had been a hallmark of her years in Washington. Despite the murmurs of protest, the move occurred and the Wildflower Center opened in its new location in 1995. Two years later, on Mrs. Johnson's eighty-fifth birthday, the trustees renamed it the Lady Bird Johnson Wildflower Center. Its membership had swelled to more than 25,000 individuals and businesses. The 42-acre site received more than 100,000 visitors annually, some of whom came to have weddings and parties on the center's grounds, where native plants and regional architecture produced a harmonious and beautiful setting. "In a way I'm smiling with pleasure and in a way I'm breathless to try to go ahead," the former First Lady said in December 1997. As her eighty-sixth birthday approached, the Wildflower Center, under its director, Dr. Robert Breunig, had become a permanent part of the Austin scene and a constructive force for the environment nationally.[44]

Throughout her eighth decade, Lady Bird Johnson spoke often of the need to reduce her schedule and cut back on her commitments. The goal was an elusive one. In 1988 she coauthored a best-selling book with Carlton Lees, *Wildflowers Across America*. That same year she received a Congressional Gold Medal, and Pres. Ronald Reagan welcomed her back to the White House.

Her eightieth birthday was a time of extended celebration at the Lyndon B. Johnson Library, as her friends assembled to recognize her life and achievements. Harry Middleton, the director of the LBJ Library, compiled *Lady Bird Johnson: A Life Well Lived* (1992), which combined her own words and the fond memories of her friends to recall the events and good causes in which she had been involved. At the end of the book, Mrs. Johnson was quoted as remarking, "There's been so much to my life, and I almost feel like pinching myself and saying, 'Did all of this happen to me?' "[45]

Yet even her vigorous energy and robust constitution could not escape the effects of her advancing years. During summer 1993 she had a slight stroke and recurring episodes of dizziness. Macular degeneration impaired her eyesight and left her legally blind. She could no longer read the books she had loved so much and had to be content with recorded versions. Her ailment did not prevent her from seeing the wildflowers in bloom in spring 1998, however, and she spoke of how in "this season of renewal, my pleasure in life soars, painting in gay abandon the landscape of my hopes for the Center and the glory of the living Earth." [46]

As her eighty-sixth birthday approached and then passed, the honors for her work accumulated. In December 1998 the LBJ Library, where her offices had been for many years, opened a permanent exhibit devoted to her life. On the one-hundredth year of its publication, *Audubon* magazine selected "100 Champions of Conservation," among whom were Lyndon and Lady Bird Johnson, "the only married couple to make the list." In mid-January 1999, Secretary of the Interior Bruce Babbitt presented Mrs. Johnson with a lifetime achievement award from the National Plant Conservation Initiative for her message that "we should appreciate the God-given beauty of our country." Mrs. Johnson told reporters, "I hope I can get to see a beautiful spring." [47]

In these twilight years she had her large family with her on many personal occasions. Grandchildren and great-grandchildren added to her pleasure as the matriarch of the Johnson family, "Nini" to the younger members of the clan. Her granddaughter, Lucinda Robb, said in a film about Mrs. Johnson for the National Park Service, "My grandmother always had a way of bringing us all home and that's what the ranch is. Whenever I think of heaven I always think it is going to be some place that looks exactly like the ranch on a beautiful spring or fall day." As Lady Bird Johnson put it, "So take care. And just savor the hour." [48]

Lady Bird Johnson's contributions to the environment have received numerous awards and recognition, including a Presidential Medal of Freedom from Gerald Ford in 1977 and a Congressional Gold Medal in 1988. What has been less appreciated was her significant role in shaping the modern institution of the First Lady. Because of the way in which Lyndon Johnson assumed the presidency and the way his administration ended, Lady Bird Johnson was overshadowed by her predecessor and also caught up in the perception that the Johnson years had been an unalloyed failure. Three decades after she left the White House, however, her contribution to the history of First Ladies is more apparent.

Lady Bird Johnson was the first activist wife of a president since Eleanor Roosevelt a generation earlier. More important, in her ap-

Lady Bird Johnson and her great-grandchildren, Tatum Rebekah Nugent
(two years old) and Johnson Saunders Covert (one year old), Christmas 1997.
(Patsy Chaney photograph)

proach to the environment and her other duties, Mrs. Johnson established the modern structure of how First Ladies operate. By
appointing Liz Carpenter as her staff director, Mrs. Johnson made
clear that the First Lady had to have bureaucratic support of her
own to get her job done. Aides for speechwriting, handling corre-

spondence, and interacting with television became commonplace for subsequent First Ladies, but Lady Bird Johnson initiated the positions.

In the substance of her actions, Mrs. Johnson put the president's wife into the policy-making process in a more direct way than any previous First Lady had ever done. She attended legislative strategy sessions, she and her staff prepared speeches for lawmakers, and she lobbied for the environmental programs that she endorsed. Although other First Ladies had backed legislative initiatives, Mrs. Johnson was the first one to have a specific law identified with her name in the Highway Beautification Act of 1965.

The extent of Lady Bird Johnson's contribution in these areas did not receive full public recognition at the time because of the efficiency and smoothness with which she went about her work. Notable in her tenure is the absence of what would become known as "flaps," embarrassing incidents that sparked press scrutiny. The Eartha Kitt episode was an exception to the generally favorable press coverage that she received from 1965 to 1969. Lady Bird Johnson carefully avoided saying that she was the presidents's partner or that the nation received two chief executives for the price of one. With her political insight, she recognized the limits that a male-centered society imposed on women in politics.

The best testament to the effectiveness of Lady Bird Johnson as First Lady was her accomplishments for the environment. Her work for beautification in Washington, DC provided a major stimulus to the improvement of the nation's capital. Around the nation, she encouraged thousands of Americans to take similar actions in their own local communities with effects that are still rippling through the United States. She was a crucial catalyst in a campaign to reduce blight on the roadsides and to restrain the spread of billboards.

Among First Ladies of the twentieth century, Lady Bird Johnson deserves to rank with Eleanor Roosevelt as one of the significant innovators in the history of the institution. Her achievements in Washington were important for the development of the role of the First Lady, and the consistency with which she pursued her vision of the environment after the White House added to her historical influence. Lady Bird Johnson explored the amorphous and ill-defined possibilities of the institution of the First Lady and stretched them into a significant campaign for an important national priority. When her opportunity came to be an advocate for the preservation and perpetuation of the nation's environment, she seized it with dedication, commitment, and lasting results. In so doing, she set a formidable standard for future First Ladies.

NOTES

ABBREVIATIONS

AF

Alphabetical File

BF

Beautification Files

GPO

Government Printing Office

HB

Highway Beautification

JHP

Johnson House Papers

LBJ

Lady Bird Johnson

LBJA

Lyndon B. Johnson Archives

LBJL

Lyndon B. Johnson Library

LC

Library of Congress, Washington, DC

LCAF

Liz Carpenter's Alphabetical File

LJ

Lyndon Johnson

NR

Natural Resources

OH

Oral History

WHCF

White House Central Files

WHNF

White House Name Files

WHSF

White House Social Files

FROM KARNACK TO THE WHITE HOUSE

1. Ruth Montgomery, "Selling the Nation on Beauty," *New York Journal American,* 30 May 1965; Jan Jarboe, "Lady Bird Looks Back," *Texas Monthly,* Dec. 1994, p. 148.

2. Nan Robertson, "Our New First Lady," *Saturday Evening Post,* 8 Feb. 1964, pp. 22–23; Antonio Taylor, Oral History (OH), Lyndon Baines Johnson Library (LBJL), 23 Nov. 1969, p. 5.

3. Harry Middleton, *Lady Bird Johnson: A Life Well Lived* (Austin, TX: Lyndon Baines Johnson Foundation, 1992), p. 43.

4. Cameron McElroy and Lucille W. McElroy, OH, 11 Mar. 1981, p. 9; Robertson, "Our New First Lady," p. 23.

5. Middleton, *Lady Bird Johnson,* p. 46.

6. Dorris Powell, OH, 18 Apr. 1978, p. 8.

7. The quotations are from a 1963 interview with Lady Bird Johnson (LBJ), apparently conducted by Blake Clark, in the Ruth Montgomery Papers, Texas Collection, Baylor University.

8. Eugenia B. Lasseter, OH, 10 Mar. 1981, p. 19 (first quotation), and Ruth Montgomery, *Mrs. LBJ* (New York: Holt, Rinehart and Winston, 1964), p. 18 (second quotation).

9. Mrs. Johnson's remarks in 1976 at the dedication of the LBJ Grove at the Lady Bird Johnson Park in Washington, DC, are in the *Congressional Record,* 94th Cong., 2d sess., 7 May 1976, extension of remarks of Cong. J. J. Pickle, p. 13033; Mrs. Lyndon B. Johnson, "Memories of the Wilderness," in *Wild Places of North America: Engagement Calendar, 1984* (Washington, DC: National Geographic Society, 1984), p. 4; Elizabeth Janeway, "The First Lady: A Professional at Getting Things Done," *Ladies Home Journal,* Apr. 1964, p. 64; Middleton, *Lady Bird Johnson,* p. 53.

10. Lady Bird Johnson, *A White House Diary* (New York: Holt, Rinehart and Winston, 1970), pp. 74, 488.

11. Montgomery, *Mrs. LBJ,* p. 14 (first quotation); LBJ to Jack R. Maguire, 18 Apr. 1966, White House Social Files (WHSF), Alphabetical File (AF), box 2022 (second quotation).

12. LBJ to Frances Davis Miller, 9 Oct. 1964, WHSF, AF, Personal Data–Education M, box 1621; "The Doors of the World Swung Open," University of Texas Ex-Students Association, *Alcade,* Nov. 1964, p. 21; Middleton, *Lady Bird Johnson,* p. 56.

13. Eugenia B. Lasseter, OH no. 1, 10 Mar. 1981, p. 5 (first quotation); Jarboe, "Lady Bird Johnson," p. 148 (second quotation); Flora Reta Schreiber, "Lady Bird Johnson's First Years of Marriage," *Woman's Day*, Dec. 1967, p. 91 (third quotation); Emily Crow Selden, OH no. 2, 16 Jan. 1980, p. 10 (fourth quotation).

14. Lady Bird Johnson interview, Montgomery Papers; a copy of her personalized stationery is on display at LBJL.

15. Marie Smith, *The President's Lady: An Intimate Biography of Mrs. Lyndon B. Johnson* (New York: Random House, 1964), pp. 40–41; Pierre van Paasen and James Waterman Wise, eds., *Naziism: An Assault on Civilization* (New York: H. Smith and R. Haas, 1934).

16. Lady Bird Johnson interview, Montgomery Papers.

17. "A National Tribute to Lady Bird Johnson on the Occasion of Her Sixty-fifth Birthday," 11 Dec. 1977, pp. 4, 6, LBJL; Johnson, *A White House Diary*, p. 604.

18. Thomas Jefferson Taylor to Ida McKay, 23 Nov. 1964, in "LBJ as a Determined Suitor," *U.S. News and World Report*, 15 Feb. 1965, p. 11.

19. Lady Bird Johnson interview, Montgomery Papers; Lasseter, OH, 10 Mar. 1981, p. 10.

20. Booth Mooney, *The Lyndon Johnson Story* (New York: Farrar, Straus, 1964), p. 21.

21. Schreiber, "Lady Bird Johnson's First Years of Marriage," p. 89; Barbara Klaw, comp., "Lady Bird Johnson Remembers," *American Heritage*, Dec. 1980, p. 13.

22. Robert Dallek, *Flawed Giant: Lyndon Johnson and His Times, 1961–1973* (New York: Oxford University Press, 1998), p. 408.

23. Nancy Dickerson, *Among Those Present: A Reporter's View of Twenty-Five Years in Washington* (New York: Random House, 1976), pp. 138–39.

24. Merle Miller, *Lyndon: An Oral Biography* (New York: Putnam's, 1980), p. 54.

25. Miller, *Lyndon*, p. 60; Katie Louchheim, ed., *The Making of the New Deal: The Insiders Speak* (Cambridge: Harvard University Press, 1983), p. 300.

26. Louchheim, ed., *Making of the New Deal*, p. 303; Miller, *Lyndon*, p. 65.

27. LBJ to Mrs. Edward Cape, 3 Mar. 1942, Lyndon B. Johnson Archives (LBJA), Edward Cape file, Selected Names, box 14; LBJ to Jerry Wilkie, 15 April 1942, Johnson House Papers (JHP), Personal Correspondence, 1942, box 37.

28. LBJ to Ben Crider, 16 July 1942, LBJA, Selected Names, box 16.

29. Ronnie Dugger, *The Politician: The Life and Times of Lyndon Johnson* (New York: Norton, 1982), p. 54.

30. LBJ to Mr. and Mrs. E. H. Perry, 22 Mar. 1943, LBJA, E. H. Perry folder, Selected Names, box 29 (first quotation); "Ways to Beautify America," *U.S. News and World Report,* 22 Feb. 1965, p. 72 (second quotation); Louchheim, ed., *Making of the New Deal,* p. 300 (last quotation).

31. Ken Givens, "A Brief History of the Early Years of One Austin Texas Radio Station, KTBC" (typescript in Center for American History, Austin, 1981), pp. 1, 4.

32. Jack Gould to author, personal comment, 1960s.

33. Speech drafts, "Future Speeches," JHP, box 54 (first quotation); Dugger, *Politician,* p. 270 (second quotation); *Wall Street Journal,* 23 Mar. 1964; Harfield Weedin, OH, 24 Feb. 1983, p. 15.

34. Givens, "Brief History," p. 4; Lyndon Johnson (LJ) to Willard Deason, 10 May 1943, JHP, Willard Deason file, box 143.

35. *Wall Street Journal,* 23 Mar. 1964; LBJ to Jesse Kellam, 6 Dec. 1963, WHSF, AF, Personal Data–S, box 1621.

36. LJ to Edward M. Cape, 21 Mar. 1944, JHP, Edward M. Cape file, box 142.

37. *Wichita Falls Record,* 24 Aug. 1948; W. H. Wentland to LJ, 6 Sept. 1948, JHP, W-Austin, box 91; Montgomery, *Mrs. LBJ,* pp. 36–37.

38. Montgomery, *Mrs. LBJ,* p. 45; Miller, *Lyndon,* p. 357.

39. LBJ to O. F. Garrett, 21 Sept. 1955, LBJA, G folder, Selected Names, box 4.

40. Interview with Dr. Dor W. Brown, 10 July 1997; Lady Bird Johnson, as told to Jack Harrison Pollack, "Help Your Husband Guard His Heart," *Dallas Morning News,* 12 Feb. 1956 (first and second quotations); LBJ to Terrell Maverick, 28 July 1955, LBJA, Maury Maverick file, Selected Names, box 27.

41. Johnson, "Help Your Husband Guard His Heart," p. 9; LBJ to Thomas G. Corcoran, 27 Aug. 1955, LBJA, Thomas G. Corcoran file, Selected Names, box 3.

42. "Mrs. Johnson Laughs at Idea of First Lady," *Washington Evening Star,* 12 Aug. 1956; Mary V. R. Thayer, "Lyndon's Holding Court," *Washington Post,* 15 Aug. 1956.

43. Gordon Langley Hall, *Lady Bird and Her Daughters* (Philadelphia: Macrae Smith, 1967), p. 154; Katie Louchheim, *By the Political Sea* (Garden City, NY; Doubleday, 1976), p. 222.

44. Montgomery, *Mrs. LBJ,* p. 75.

45. Alfred Steinberg, *Sam Johnson's Boy* (New York: Macmillan, 1968), p. 529 (first quotation); Theodore H. White, *The Making of the President, 1964* (New York: Atheneum, 1965), p. 414 (second quotation); Smith, *The President's Lady,* p. 136.

46. U.S. Senate, *Congressional Record,* 86th Cong., 2d sess., 24 Aug. 1960, p. 17397.

47. Montgomery, *Mrs. LBJ*, p. 89 (first quotation), p. 83 (second quotation); Steinberg, *Sam Johnson's Boy*, p. 540 (last quotation).

48. LBJ interview, Montgomery Papers; Miller, *Lyndon*, p. 271; Smith, *President's Lady*, p. 126 (first quotation); Montgomery, *Mrs. LBJ*, p. 101 (second quotation).

49. Hall, *Lady Bird and Her Daughters*, p. 161 (first quotation); Montgomery, *Mrs. LBJ*, p. 143 (second quotation).

50. Liz Carpenter, *Ruffles and Flourishes* (1969; rpt., College Station: Texas A&M University Press, 1993), pp. 28–29; Bess Abell, OH, 28 May 1969, pp. 4–7.

51. Smith, *President's Lady*, pp. 163, 171.

52. U.S. Senate, *Congressional Record*, 88th Cong., lst sess., 13 Dec. 1963, p. 24509; Smith, *President's Lady*, p. 185 (first quotation); Blake Clark, "Lyndon Johnson's Lady Bird," *Reader's Digest*, Dec. 1963, p. 112.

53. Montgomery, *Mrs. LBJ*, p. 141 (first quotation) and p. 160 (last quotation); the *Post* editorial appears in U.S. Senate, *Congressional Record*, 88th Cong., 1st sess., 12 May 1963, p. 9444.

54. Clark, "Lyndon Johnson's Lady Bird," p. 112.

BECOMING FIRST LADY

1. Lady Bird Johnson, *A White House Diary* (New York: Holt, Rinehart and Winston, 1970), p. 6 (first and second quotations); Marie Smith, *The President's Lady: An Intimate Biography of Mrs. Lyndon B. Johnson* (New York: Random House, 1964), p. 19 (third quotation).

2. Johnson, *A White House Diary*, p. 10.

3. Ibid., p. 15.

4. Ibid., p. 37.

5. Nan Robertson is quoted in Myra G. Gutin, *The President's Partner: The First Lady in the Twentieth Century* (New York: Greenwood Press, 1989), p. 120; Liz Carpenter, *Ruffles and Flourishes* (College Station: Texas A&M University Press, 1993), p. 117.

6. Johnson, *A White House Diary*, p. vii (first quotation), and "About the Author: A Reminiscence," in *A White House Diary: The Exhibition*, p. 78 (second and third quotations).

7. Ruth Montgomery, *Mrs. LBJ* (New York: Holt, Rinehart and Winston, 1964), p. 152.

8. Montgomery, *Mrs. LBJ*, p. 152.

9. Johnson, *A White House Diary*, p. 347; Lady Bird Johnson visited my seminar on First Ladies in November 1982.

10. Horace Busby to Liz Carpenter, 7 Jan. 1965, "Memos for Liz Carpen-

ter," box 18, Horace Busby office files. Mrs. Johnson did send a friendly letter to Margaret Sanger in 1966 (Ellen Chesler, *Woman of Valor: Margaret Sanger and the Birth Control Movement in America* [New York: Simon and Schuster, 1992], p. 467).

11. *Addresses by the First Lady: Mrs. Lyndon Baines Johnson, 1964,* pamphlet in LBJL, p. 24; Joseph Califano, *The Triumph and Tragedy of Lyndon Johnson* (New York: Simon and Schuster, 1991), p. 208.

12. Johnson, *A White House Diary,* p. 349 (first quotation), and p. 351 (second quotation).

13. Michael R. Beschloss, ed., *Taking Charge: The Johnson White House Tapes, 1963–1964* (New York: Simon and Schuster, 1997), pp. 272–73.

14. Merle Miller, *Lyndon: An Oral Biography* (New York: Putnam's, 1980), pp. 354–55; Richard "Cactus" Pryor is quoted in the script for the film on Lady Bird Johnson by Thaxton Green Studios, shown at the Lyndon B. Johnson National Park site in Johnson City, Texas. His remarks appear on p. 32 of the final version of the script.

15. Katie Louchheim, "Her Interest Is People," *Ladies Home Journal,* Mar. 1964, pp. 56, 126; Ruth Montgomery, "What Kind of Woman Is Our New First Lady?" *Good Housekeeping,* Mar. 1964, p. 44.

16. Barbara Klaw, comp., "Lady Bird Johnson Remembers," *American Heritage,* Dec. 1980, pp. 7–8; Katie Louchheim, ed., *The Making of the New Deal: The Insiders Speak* (Cambridge: Harvard University Press, 1983), p. 304; Johnson, *White House Diary,* p. 106.

17. Marianne Means, *The Woman in the White House* (New York: Random House, 1963), p. 248 (quotation).

18. "I Don't Consider Myself Dull at All: The Real Lady Bird Johnson," *National Observer,* 24 Apr. 1967.

19. Johnson, *White House Diary,* p. 10.

20. "Mrs. Lyndon B. Johnson's Remarks at Wilkes College, Wilkes-Barre, Pennsylvania, January 11, 1964," (first quotation), WHSF, Liz Carpenter's subject files, Trip to Wilkes-Barre, box 1; Johnson, *White House Diary,* p. 38 (second quotation); "First Lady on the Move: Schedule Stirs Memories of Eleanor Roosevelt," *U.S. News and World Report,* 27 Jan. 1964, p. 16.

21. Johnson, *White House Diary,* pp. 99, 141, 159–60.

22. *Addresses by the First Lady, Mrs. Lyndon Baines Johnson, 1964,* pamphlet in LBJL, pp. 3, 11.

23. "Lady Bird's Pine Lands and Her Tenants," *U.S. News and World Report,* 4 May 1964, pp. 43–45; Beschloss, ed., *Taking Charge,* p. 353; Johnson, *White House Diary,* p. 103.

24. LBJ to L. L. Camp, 11 Feb. 1964, White House Central Files (WHCF), EX/PP16, Trees Planted, box 126; Stewart Udall to LBJ, 24 July 1964, WHSF, AF, Stewart Udall, box 2016; "Mrs. Johnson Opens the American Landmarks Celebration," press release, 4 Aug. 1964, WHCF, PP5/LBJ, box 62.

25. Johnson, *White House Diary,* p. 166.

26. *Addresses by the First Lady,* pp. 5, 18–19.

27. *Public Papers of the Presidents of the United States: Lyndon B. Johnson, 1963–1964,* 2 vols. (Washington, DC: GPO, 1965), 1:357.

28. Charles M. Haar, OH, no. 1, 14 June 1971, p. 4 (first quotation); Richard Goodwin, "Preservation of Natural Beauty," 17 June 1964, Stewart Udall Papers, University of Arizona Library, Tucson.

29. Udall to LJ, 27 Nov. 1963, WHCF, Legislation/Natural Resources, 22 Nov. 1963–20 Oct. 1964, box 142.

30. Hal K. Rothman, *The Greening of a Nation? Environmentalism in the United States Since 1945* (Fort Worth, TX: Harcourt Brace, 1998), pp. 7–55.

31. Rothman, *Greening,* pp. 83–101; Linda Lear, *Rachel Carson, Witness for Nature* (New York: Henry Holt, 1997).

32. James Reston, Jr. to Udall, 5 Aug. 1964, Udall Papers.

33. Stewart Udall to Lewis L. Gould, 1 Oct. 1984; Gould interview with Udall, 11 Apr. 1984; Gould interview with LBJ, 16 Sept. 1984.

34. Reston to Udall, 5 Aug. 1964, Udall Papers; Haar, OH, 14 June 1971, pp. 13, 22.

35. Stewart Udall, *The Quiet Crisis* (New York: Holt, Rinehart and Winston, 1963), p. viii.

36. Udall interview, 11 Apr. 1984; Udall, OH, 19 May 1969, p. 1.

37. Udall, OH, 19 May 1969, p. 7; Martin V. Melosi, "Lyndon Johnson and Environmental Policy," in *The Johnson Years,* ed. Robert A. Divine, vol. 2 (Lawrence: University Press of Kansas, 1987), p. 121.

38. Udall to Liz Carpenter, 23 Apr. 1964, LBJ to Udall, 31 July, 1964, Udall Papers; Udall interview, 11 Apr. 1984.

39. *Salt Lake City Tribune,* 16 Aug. 1964 (University of Utah quotation); draft of Flaming Gorge speech, WHSF, Liz Carpenter subject file, Western Trip, box 9; Udall to LJ, 19 Aug. 1964, LJ to Udall, 24 Aug. 1964, WHCF, EX/PP5/LBJ, 15 July 1964–Oct. 1964, box 62; Udall interview, 11 Apr. 1984 (for the tour de force comment).

40. Udall interview, 11 Apr. 1984 (first three quotations), and Udall, OH, 19 May 1969, p. 12.

41. Johnson, *White House Diary,* p. 192 (first three quotations); Miller, *Lyndon,* p. 391 (other quotations); Beschloss, ed., *Taking Charge,* p. 534.

42. India Edwards to Liz Carpenter, 9 Sept. 1964, WHSF, Liz Carpenter's subject file, Whistle Stop, box 11.

43. Jan Jarboe, "Lady Bird Looks Back," *Texas Monthly,* Dec. 1994, p. 148.

44. Zephyr Wright recounts the motel episode in OH, 5 Dec. 1974, p. 6; Carpenter, *Ruffles and Flourishes,* pp. 147–48.

45. Carpenter, *Ruffles and Flourishes,* p. 143 (first quotation), pp. 147–48 (second quotation); Johnson, *White House Diary,* p. 195.

46. Carpenter, *Ruffles and Flourishes,* pp. 153–58; Miller, *Lyndon,* pp. 396–97.

47. Carpenter, *Ruffles and Flourishes,* p. 155 (first quotation); p. 158 (second quotation); Gutin, *The President's Partner,* p. 117; Norma Ruth Holly Foreman, "The First Lady as a Leader of Public Opinion: A Study of the Role and Press Relations of Lady Bird Johnson" (Ph.D diss., University of Texas, Austin, 1971), p. 171 (Boggs quotation).

48. Foreman, "First Lady as Leader of Public Opinion," p. 173 (first quotation), p. 174 (third and fourth quotations); Carpenter, *Ruffles and Flourishes,* p. 162 (second quotation).

49. Doris Fleeson, "Mrs. Johnson Draws the Names," *Washington Evening Star,* 8 Oct. 1964; Johnson, *White House Diary,* p. 198.

50. Liz Carpenter, OH, 27 Aug. 1969, pp. 32–39; Miller, *Lyndon,* p. 604 (LBJ's statement).

51. Johnson, *White House Diary,* p. 198.

52. Lady Bird Johnson, *Texas: A Roadside View* (San Antonio, TX: Trinity University Press, 1980), p. xviii.

WAYS TO BEAUTIFY AMERICA

1. Harry Middleton, *Lady Bird Johnson: A Life Well Lived* (Austin: Lyndon Baines Johnson Foundation, 1992), p. 89; LBJ to Betty Friedan, 13 Feb. 1965, WHSF, Project Head Start, box 1705; John C. O'Brien, "First Lady to Spark 'Project Head Start' for Deprived Pupils," *Philadelphia Inquirer,* 28 Feb. 1965.

2. Sargent Shriver to LBJ, 1 March 1965, WHSF, Sargent Shriver, box 1848.

3. Lady Bird Johnson, *A White House Diary* (New York: Holt, Rinehart and Winston, 1970), p. 310; Shriver to LBJ, 1 Dec. 1965, WHSF, Sargent Shriver, box 1848.

4. LBJ to Shriver, 30 June 1966, WHSF, Liz Carpenter's files, Project Head Start, Box 97; Shriver to LBJ, 16 Apr. 1968, WHSF, Sargent Shriver, Box 1848. For more on Lady Bird Johnson's role with Head Start, see Laura Susan Beilharz, "The Unique Influence and Tremendous Impact of Mrs. Lyndon Baines Johnson on Operation Head Start" (seminar paper, University of Texas at Austin, 1986).

5. Henry Brandon, "A Talk with the First Lady," *New York Times Magazine,* 10 Sept. 1967.

6. Stewart Udall, "Memorandum for the First Lady," 19 Nov. 1964, Udall Papers (first quotation); Udall interview, 11 Apr. 1984 (second quotation).

7. Elizabeth Rowe to LBJ, 8 Dec. 1964, with Rowe to Ashton Gonella, 8 Dec. 1964, Formation of Committee, WHSF/BF, box 1.

8. Katie Louchheim, "Suggested Program for Mrs. Johnson," 20 Nov. 1964, "National Beautification," 20 Nov. 1964, box C33; Stewart Udall, "Memorandum for the First Lady: Proposed Capital Beautification Program," 9 Dec. 1964; and Antonia Chayes to LBJ, 9 Dec. 1964, all in papers of Katherine Louchheim, Library of Congress (LC), Manuscripts Division, box C29; Antonia Chayes to Lewis L. Gould, 6 Oct. 1986.

9. "Informal Notes of Conversation in the White House with Mrs. Johnson," 11 Dec. 1964, and "Luncheon Notes," 15 Dec. 1964, Louchheim Papers, box C29.

10. Udall, "Memorandum for the First Lady," 9 Dec. 1964, Louchheim Papers, box C29; Wolf Von Eckardt, "Washington's Chance for Splendor," *Harper's Magazine,* Sept. 1963, p. 55.

11. Andrew Kopkind and James Rodgeway, "Washington: The Lost Colony," *New Republic,* 23 Apr. 1964, p. 13 (lost colony), and p. 24 (Kennedy remark).

12. For the origins of highway beautification, see chapter 5.

13. *Public Papers of the Presidents of the United States: Lyndon B. Johnson, 1965,* 2 vols. (Washington, DC: GPO, 1966), 1:8; Maxine Cheshire, "Mrs. Johnson Digs New Landscape Role on Capitol Hill," *Washington Post,* 5 Jan. 1965; Lady Bird Johnson, *A White House Diary* (New York: Holt, Rinehart and Winston, 1970), p. 215.

14. LBJ to Mary Lasker, 30 Jan. 1965, WHSF, AF, Beautification, L folder, box 12; Johnson, *White House Diary,* p. 234.

15. *Public Papers,* 1: 155, 156.

16. Johnson, *White House Diary,* pp. 240–42.

17. "Ways to Beautify America: Exclusive Interview with the First Lady," *U.S. News and World Report,* 22 Feb. 1965, pp. 72, 74, 75, 78.

18. Eileen Boone to LJ, 5 Feb. 1965, Mrs. Clifford Norman to LJ, 22 Feb. 1965, WHCF, Natural Resources (NR), 1 Dec. 1964–30 Apr. 1965, box 6; James Perry, "Natural Beauty Is a Political Natural," *National Observer,* 1 Mar. 1965.

19. Wolf Von Eckardt, *A Place to Live: The Crisis of the Cities* (New York: Dell, 1967), p. 25.

20. William H. Wilson, "J. Horace McFarland and the City Beautiful Movement," *Journal of Urban History* 7 (May 1981): 315.

21. Ibid., p. 318.

22. Martin V. Melosi, *Garbage in the Cities: Refuse, Reform and the Environment, 1880–1980* (College Station: Texas A&M University Press, 1981), p. 128.

23. Barbara Klaw, comp., "Lady Bird Johnson Remembers," *American Heritage,* Dec. 1980, p. 6.

24. Sharon Francis, OH, 20 May 1969, p. 35; Liz Carpenter, OH, 4 Apr. 1969, p. 11; Charles M. Haar, OH, 14 June 1971, pp. 10, 11.

25. Lady Bird Johnson, "Beautification and Public Welfare," *Social Action* 34 (May 1968): 11.

26. LBJ to Sylvia Porter, 28 Dec. 1965, WHSF, Liz Carpenter's Alphabetical File (LCAF), Beautification-P, box 14.

27. Sharon Francis, OH, 20 May 1969, pp. 2, 7.

28. Ibid., pp. 8–12, 17; LBJ to Francis, 10 Mar. 1965, WHSF, AF, Stewart Udall, box 2016.

29. Cynthia Wilson, interview, 24 Oct. 1985.

30. Johnson, *White House Diary,* pp. 248–49.

31. "Beautification Summary: The Committee for a More Beautiful Capital, 1965–1968," LBJL, p. 9.

32. Carpenter, *Ruffles and Flourishes,* p. 74; Johnson, *White House Diary,* pp. 270–73.

33. Johnson, *White House Diary,* p. 271.

34. Ibid., *White House Diary,* pp. 274, 275–76.

35. Mary Lasker to Katie Louchheim, 12 Oct. 1965 (quotation), box C29, Louchheim Papers.

36. Stewart Udall, Suggestions Concerning the President's White House Conference on Natural Beauty, 19 Jan. 1965, John Macy files, White House Conference on Natural Beauty, box 891; Johnson, *White House Diary,* p. 234.

37. Nathaniel Alexander Owings, *The Spaces in Between: An Architect's Journey* (Boston: Houghton Mifflin, 1973), p. 169; Robin W. Winks, *Laurance S. Rockefeller: Catalyst for Conservation* (Washington, DC: Island Press, 1997).

38. James L. Sundquist, *Politics and Policy: The Eisenhower, Kennedy and Johnson Years* (Washington, DC: Brookings Institution, 1968), p. 355.

39. Laurance S. Rockefeller, "Business and Beauty: Our Changing Landscape," *Vital Speeches of the Day* 15 (Jan. 1966): 220.

40. John R. Churchill to Chief of Office of Legislation and Cooperative Relations, 11 Feb. 1965, Records of the Department of the Interior, reel 30 (first

and second quotations); Jack Valenti to LJ, 4 Mar. 1965, WHCF/NR, MC, box 8; Rockefeller to LBJ, 19 Mar. 1965, WHSF, AF, Laurance Rockefeller, box 1779.

41. *Beauty for America: Proceedings of the White House Conference on Natural Beauty* (Washington, DC: GPO, 1965), pp. 20, 68.

42. Ibid., p. 689.

43. Ibid., pp. 17, 19, 21, 22.

44. Oral Kelly and Roberta Hornig, "Fight for Natural Beauty: Delegates to Ask President," *Washington Evening Star,* 25 May 1965 (first quotation); *Beauty for America,* pp. 481–82 (McHarg), and p. 527 (Halprin).

45. *Beauty for America,* pp. 676, 679, 681; Larry Fuller, ed., *The Land, the City, and the Human Spirit: America the Beautiful: An Assessment* (Austin, TX: Lyndon Baines Johnson Library, 1985), p. 1.

46. LBJ to William L. Rutherford, 24 June 1965, WHSF, AF, Beautification-Ford, box 113 (first and second quotations); Joseph Watterson, "Beauty USA: The White House Conference on Natural Beauty," *AIA Journal* (July 1965): 61–62; *National Wildlife* 3 (April/May 1965): 29.

47. Fuller, ed., *The Land, the City, and the Human Spirit,* pp. xix, 2.

BEAUTIFYING THE TWO WASHINGTONS

1. Katie Louchheim, *By the Political Sea* (Garden City, NY: Doubleday, 1970), p. 232.

2. John Gunther, *Taken at the Flood: The Story of Albert D. Lasker* (New York: Harper, 1960), pp. 240–41.

3. "Lady Philanthropist: Mrs. Albert D. Lasker," U.S. Senate, *Congressional Record, Appendix,* 85th Cong., 1st sess., 17 June 1957, p. A4753; Samuel Grafton, "Cities in Bloom," *Reader's Digest,* July 1960, pp. 108–10.

4. Nash Castro, OH, 25 Feb. 1969, p. 2 (quotation); Johnson, *White House Diary,* p. 318.

5. Lady Bird Johnson, *A White House Diary* (New York: Holt, Rinehart and Winston, 1970), p. 238.

6. Castro to LBJ, 13 Oct. 1965 (first quotation), Castro to Sutton Jett, 6 Oct. and 18 Nov. 1965 (third and fourth quotations), Nash Castro Papers, Mrs. Johnson's file, box 3; Castro to Jett, 22 Oct. 1965, Stewart Udall Papers (second quotation).

7. Udall to LBJ, Dec. 1965, WHSF, AF, Stewart Udall, box 216, "Beautification Summary," p. 22.

8. Castro to LBJ, 2 Nov. 1966, Castro Papers, Mrs. Johnson's file, box 3; Transcript of Beautification Meeting, 30 Nov. 1966, WHSF/BF, box 2, pp. 11, 13, 15.

9. Lasker to Douglass Cater, 30 Jan. 1967, Douglass Cater files, Highway Beautification (HB), box 96.

10. Castro to Jett, 27 June 1967, Castro Papers, Mrs. Johnson's file, box 3.

11. U.S. House, *Department of the Interior and Related Agencies for 1968: Hearings Before a Subcommittee of the Committee on Appropriations,* 90th Cong., 1st sess. (Washington, DC: GPO, 1967), p. 345.

12. "No More Money: Julia Balks Beautification," clipping from Vancouver, WA, newspapers, dated 12 Aug. 1967, Castro Papers, Beautification file, box 7.

13. Liz Carpenter and Nash Castro to LBJ, 29 Aug. 1967, Mrs. Johnson's file, box 3.

14. Julia B. Hansen to LJ, 27 Sept. 1967, LBJ to Hansen, 6 Oct. 1967, WHCF, Gen PP5/LBJ, 16 July 1966–, box 65.

15. U.S. House, *Department of the Interior and Related Agencies Appropriations for 1969: Hearings Before a Subcommittee of the Committee on Appropriations,* 90th Cong., 2d sess. (Washington, DC: GPO, 1968), p. 506.

16. Ibid., pp. 399, 500, 501.

17. Mary Lasker to LBJ, 26 Feb. 1968, LBJ to Lasker, 29 Feb. 1968, WHSF/ Beautification Files (BF), Street Trees, box 8.

18. Barry Hyams, *Hirshhorn: Medici from Brooklyn* (New York: Dutton, 1979), pp. 142, 143, 144.

19. Ibid., pp. 149, 151, 152; Harry McPherson to LJ, 14 Sept. 1965, Harry McPherson's files, H Correspondence, box 47.

20. Hyams, *Hirshhorn,* p. 188.

21. Nathaniel Alexander Owings, *The Spaces in Between: An Architect's Journey* (Boston: Houghton Mifflin, 1973), p. 233.

22. Ibid., p. 230.

23. Ibid., pp. 233–34.

24. Transcript of Meeting, First Lady's Committee for a More Beautiful Capital, 24 Sept. 1965, WHSF/BF, box 1, pp. 36, 37–38, 61, 64.

25. Udall to Liz Carpenter, 1 Mar. 1966, Udall Papers.

26. Nathaniel Alexander Owings, *The American Aesthetic* (New York: Harper and Row, 1969), p. 93.

27. Remarks of Walter Washington at the First Lady's Beautification Luncheon, 17 Apr. 1968, WHSF/BF, Mayor's Remarks, box 6.

28. Antonia Chayes to LBJ, 9 Dec. 1964, LC, MsD, Katie Louchheim Papers, box C29.

29. "Walter Washington: Black Mayor, White Mind," in *Hustlers and Heroes: An American Political Panorama,* ed. Milton Viorst (New York: Simon and Schuster, 1971), pp. 250–51.

30. "Walter Edward Washington," *Current Biography 1968*, p. 422; Johnson, *White House Diary*.

31. Interview with Walter Washington, 9 Aug. 1984; Transcript, Meeting of First Lady's Committee for a More Beautiful Capital, 8 Apr. 1965, WHSF/BF, box 1, pp. 35, 36.

32. Walter Washington to LBJ, 24 Sept. 1965, WHSF/BF, Beautification Meeting, 24 Sept. 1965, box 1.

33. LBJ to John Hatcher, 19 Mar. 1965, WHSF/BF, Walker-Jones Beautification, box 21.

34. Washington to LBJ, 24 Sept. 1965, WHSF/BF, Beautification Meeting, 24 Sept. 1965, box 1.

35. Katharine Graham to LBJ, 28 Sept. 1965, Louchheim Papers, box C29.

36. Washington to Liz Carpenter, 20 Oct. 1965, WHSF/BF, Give Till Its Beautiful, box 6; Nash Castro to Sutton Jett, Castro Papers, Mrs. Johnson's file, box 3,

37. Polly Shackleton to LBJ, 21 Jan. 1966, WHSF, AF, Polly Shackleton, box 1836; LBJ to Shackleton, 26 Jan. 1966.

38. Project Pride, press release, 19 July 1966, Louchheim Papers, box C30; Sharon Francis to Liz Carpenter, 25 Aug. 1966, WHSF/BF, Beautification Meeting, 5 Oct. 1966, box 2.

39. Transcript, First Lady's Committee, 5 Oct. 1966, pp. 23, 24, 34, 35.

40. Shackleton to Carolyn Fortas, 20 Oct. 1966, WHSF, AF, Polly Shackleton, box 1836; Shackleton to Francis, 14 Apr. 1967, WHSF/BF, Trailblazers, box 8.

41. Joseph Judge, "New Grandeur for Flowering Washington," *National Geographic*, Apr. 1967, p. 520.

42. Sharon Francis, OH, 4 June 1969, pp. 18–19.

43. Roberta Hornig, "Stress on Neighborhood Slated in Beautification," *Washington Evening Star*, 12 Jan. 1967.

44. Castro to George B. Hartzog, 1 Apr. 1968, Castro Papers, Mrs. Johnson's file, box 3.

45. Johnson, *White House Diary*, p. 647.

46. Ibid., p. 655; Francis, OH, 27 June 1969, p. 5.

47. Lady Bird Johnson's remarks, WHSF/BF, Luncheon, Bus Tour, 17 Apr. 1968, box 4.

48. Speech of Walter Washington, WHSF/BF, Mayor's Remarks, 17 Apr. 1968, box 6; Francis, OH, 27 June 1969, p. 10; Johnson, *White House Diary*, p. 667.

49. Speech of Walter Washington, box 6.

50. *Gold Medals to the Daughter of Harry S. Truman; Lady Bird Johnson; and the Widow of Roy Wilkins: Hearing Before the Subcommittee on Consumer Affairs*

and *Coinage of the Committee on Banking, Finance, and Urban Affairs, House of Representatives*, 98th Cong., 2d sess. (Washington, DC: GPO, 1984), pp. 36, 58.

BEAUTIFYING THE HIGHWAYS

1. John Miller, "You Still Can't See Forest for the Billboards," *New York Times*, 28 Jan. 1985.

2. *Beauty for America: Proceedings of the White House Conference on Natural Beauty* (Washington, DC: GPO, 1965), p. 251.

3. Arthur C. Perry to Paul Middleton, 7 Oct. 1959, Senate subject files, Highways, 1959, with the resolution of the Outdoor Advertising Association of Texas conveyed by Middleton to LJ, 29 Sept. 1959, Senate subject files, box 677.

4. Peter Blake, *God's Own Junkyard: The Planned Deterioration of the American Landscape* (New York: Holt, Rinehart and Winston, 1964), p. 15; Charles Stevenson, "The Great Billboard Scandal of 1960," *Reader's Digest*, Mar. 1960, pp. 146–56.

5. Maxine Cheshire, "Mrs. Johnson Digs New Landscape Role on Capitol Hill," *Washington Post*, 5 Jan. 1965.

6. Phillip Tocker interview, 8 Feb. 1984; Bill Moyers, *Listening to America: A Traveler Rediscovers His Country* (New York: Harper's Magazine Press Book, 1971), p. 267.

7. *Public Papers of the Presidents of the United States: Lyndon B. Johnson, 1965*, 2 vols. (Washington, DC: GPO, 1966), 1: 18, 81.

8. "Ways to Beautify America," *U.S. News and World Report*, 22 Feb. 1965, p. 75; LBJ to Mrs. Baker Brownell, 26 Mar. 1965, WHSF, AF, Billboards-B, box 222.

9. Henry Wilson to Lawrence F. O'Brien, 16 Apr. 1965, Michael Manatos files, HB, box 8.

10. *Beauty for America*, p. 681; Tocker interview, 8 Feb. 1984.

11. For examples of opposition to the bill among conservationists, see Jack B. Robertson and Robert Evans to LJ, 26 May 1965, Fred Farr to LJ, 27 May 1965, Alan Boyd Papers, box 15. For probillboard sentiment, see James Schall to LBJ, 19 July 1965, Boyd Papers, box 16.

12. LBJ to Walter Reuther, 26 Aug. 1965, WHSF/BF, Beautification Special, box 15.

13. Elizabeth Brenner Drew, "Lady Bird's Beauty Bill," *Atlantic*, Dec. 1965, p. 71; the quotation of the president is from the Johnson slide presentation, courtesy of LBJL.

14. Liz Carpenter's comments during my interview with Mrs. Johnson, 16

Sept, 1984; Jake Jacobsen to LJ, 11 Sept. 1965, WHCF, HI3, 11 Sept. 1965–30 Mar. 1966, box 5.

15. Mike Manatos to Lawrence O'Brien, 17 Sept. 1965, Manatos files, HB, box 8.

16. Alan Boyd to Moyers and O'Brien, 23 Sept. 1965, Boyd Papers, box 17.

17. *Washington Post,* 30 Sept. 1965; LBJ to Mrs. Leonard Fox and family, 17 Sept. 1965, WHSF, AF, Beautification-Fox, box 113; Carpenter to LBJ, 4 Oct. 1965, WHSF/BF, Highway Beautification Act, box 14.

18. LBJ to Helen Reynolds, 7 Oct. 1965, WHSF, AF, Billboards-C, box 222; Carpenter to LJ, 6 Oct. 1965, WHCF, HI3, 11 Sept. 1965–30 Mar. 1966, box 6; *Washington Post,* 6 Oct. 1965 (last two quotations).

19. *Washington Post,* 8 Oct. 1965; President Johnson's comments can be heard on "A Salute to Congress, the White House," 7 Oct. 1965 (Washington, DC: White House Historical Association, 1965), phonograph record, end of side two.

20. U.S. House, *Congressional Record,* 89th Cong., 1st sess., 7 Oct. 1965, p. 26288 (first quotation), p. 26307 (second quotation), p. 26306, Dole amendment.

21. Paul Southwick to John T. Connor, 22 Oct. 1965, Department of Commerce Records, reel 1; *Public Papers, 1965,* 2: 1073; LBJ to Robert Amick, 19 Nov. 1965, WHSF, AF, Beautification–Four-H Clubs, box 113.

22. *Washington Evening Star,* 8 Oct. 1965; "Highways Not Low Ways," *Christian Science Monitor,* 20 Oct. 1965; for the cartoon, see LBJ to William H. Crawford, with a copy of the drawing as it appeared in the *Pittsburgh Press,* 11 Oct. 1965, LCAF, Beautification-P, box 14.

23. Lee Ray Page to LJ, 10 Sept. 1965, WHCF, NR, 1 Oct. 1965–8 Dec. 1966, box 7; "Apologies to Lady Bird Johnson," *Congressional Record,* 13 Oct. 1965, p. 26860; the Mauldin cartoon appears in "Signs Along the Road," *New Republic,* 2 Oct. 1965, p. 7.

24. U.S. House, *Congressional Record,* 8 Oct. 1965, p. 26423; Marsha Mercer, "Looking at Dole's Long, Long Record," www.jrnl.com/news/96/Oct/jrn6781096.html, traces how the Clinton campaign used the episode in the 1996 election.

25. Lady Bird Johnson, *A White House Diary* (New York: Holt, Rinehart and Winston, 1970), p. 325.

26. U.S. House, *Congressional Record,* 89th Cong., 2d sess., 31 Aug. 1966, p. 21340.

27. Richard D. McCarthy to Liz Carpenter, 12 May 1967, Douglass Cater

files, HB, box 96; Charles Vanik to LBJ, 25 Aug. 1967, WHSF, BF, HB, Implementation, box 16; Marjorie Hunter, "Road Beauty Law Menaced in House," *New York Times,* 4 Mar. 1967.

28. William Pearce to Culp Kruger, 28 Feb. 1966, WHCF, HI3, 15 Sept. 1965, box 5; Carpenter to Lou Canaly, 28 Mar. 1967, and Ashton Gonella to Cynthia Wilson, 6 May 1967, WHSF, LCAF, Beautification-C, box 10.

29. Carpenter to Douglass Cater, 31 Aug. 1967, WHSF/BF, Highway Beauty Act, 1967, box 15.

30. Drew Pearson, "The Lobby Against Beauty," *Washington Post,* 10 Sept. 1967; Barefoot Sanders to LJ, 2 Nov. 1967, with cover remarks by the president, Beautification, Barefoot Sanders Papers, box 16.

31. Sharon Francis, OH, 27 June 1969, pp. 44–45, 49.

32. Francis to Liz Carpenter, 8 Apr. 1965, WHSF/BF, Freeways: Routing and Design, box 10; U.S. Senate, *Congressional Record,* 89th Cong., 2d sess., 25 Feb. 1966, p. 4177.

33. Sharon Francis to Rai Okamoto, 1 Feb. 1967, WHSF/BF, Freeways: Routing and Design, box 10; W. Marvin Watson to Robert Stein, 17 July 1967, quoting LBJ, WHCF, PP5/LBJ, box 63.

34. Lady Bird Johnson, *Texas: A Roadside View* (San Antonio, TX: Trinity University Press, 1981), p. xviii.

35. U.S. Senate, *Federal Highway Beautification Assistance Act of 1979: Hearings Before the Committee on Transportation of the Committee on Environment and Public Works of the United States Senate,* 96th Cong., 1st sess. (Washington, DC: GPO, 1979), p. 42.

36. Ibid., pp. 310, 311; LBJ and Laurance Rockefeller to Sen. Slade Gorton, U.S. Senate, *Congressional Record,* 99th Cong., 2d sess., 23 Sept. 1986, p. S13263.

37. Bob Bryant and Bonnie L. Harper-Lore, "Where Flowers Bloom, So Does Hope," *Public Roads Online,* www.tfhrc.gov/pubrds/pr 97-12.

HER SPACE IN THE WORLD

1. "Beautification Summary: The Committee for a More Beautiful Capital, 1965–1968," pp. 16–18 (Sept. 1965); "First Lady Addresses Williams College," U.S. House, *Congressional Record,* 90th Cong., 1st Sess., 9 Oct. 1967, p. 28166.

2. Liz Carpenter, OH, 15 May 1969, p. 19; for the song, see Carpenter to Nash Castro, n.d., Castro Papers, "This Is Our Country," (folder title), box 11.

3. Liz Carpenter, *Ruffles and Flourishes* (College Station: Texas A&M University Press, 1993), p. 88.

4. Lady Bird Johnson, *A White House Diary* (New York: Holt, Rinehart and Winston, 1970), pp. 575, 576, 577, 578.

5. Ibid., pp. 579, 581.

6. Adam Rumoshosky speech, First Lady's Committee, Transcript of the Meeting, 28 Feb. 1966, p. 34, WHSF/BF, box 1.

7. Paul S. Forbes to Sharon Francis, 15 Oct. 1968, WHSF/BF, Report to the President, box 12.

8. *Public Papers of the Presidents of the United States: Lyndon B. Johnson, 1966*, 2 vols. (Washington, DC: GPO, 1967), 2: 1457.

9. Sharon Francis to Udall, 18 Aug. 1966, Stewart Udall Papers.

10. *Public Papers, 1966*, 1: 195, 203.

11. Johnson, *White House Diary*, pp. 317–18.

12. Ibid., pp. 518–19.

13. Ibid., pp. 611–12.

14. Ibid., pp. 616–21.

15. Ibid., p. 622.

16. Ibid., pp. 622.

17. Ibid., pp. 622–23; Eartha Kitt, *Alone with Me* (Chicago: Henry Regnery, 1976), pp. 246–47.

18. "A Word from Miss Kitt," *Newsweek*, 29 Jan. 1968.

19. Johnson, *White House Diary*, pp. 623–24; Janet Mezzack, " 'Without manners you are nothing': Lady Bird Johnson, Eartha Kitt, and the 'Women Doers' Luncheon of January 18, 1968," *Presidential Studies Quarterly* 20 (fall 1990): 745–61.

20. Johnson, *White House Diary*, pp. 645–46; Jan Jarboe, "Lady Bird Looks Back," *Texas Monthly*, Dec. 1994, p. 117 (LBJ and television).

21. "Beautification Summary," pp. 79–80.

22. *Public Papers of the Presidents of the United States: Lyndon B. Johnson, 1968–1969*, 2 vols. (Washington, DC: GPO, 1969), 2: 808–9; LBJ interview, 16 Sept. 1984.

23. Matthew Nimetz to Joseph Califano, 31 July 1968, James Gaither files, Beautification, box 257.

24. Califano to LBJ, 30 Sept. 1968, WHCF, NR, 1 July 1968–, box 6.

25. Castro to George B. Hartzog, 1 Oct. 1968, Castro Papers, Mrs. Johnson's file, box 3; Johnson, *White House Diary*, pp. 714–15; Francis, OH, 27 June 1969, p. 60.

26. Johnson, *White House Diary*, p. 725.

27. Ibid., pp. 735–37.

28. Shana Alexander, "Best First Lady," *Life*, 13 Dec. 1968, p. 226; "Lady Beautiful," *Christian Century*, 27 Nov. 1968, p. 1523.

29. Thaxton Green Studios, "Lady Bird Johnson," script, pp. 35–36.

30. Castro to George B. Hartzog, 18 Dec. 1968, Castro Papers, Mrs. Johnson's file, box 3; Francis, OH, 27 June 1969, pp. 68–72.

31. Johnson, *White House Diary,* p. 783.

32. U.S. Senate, *Congressional Record,* 91st Cong., 1st sess., 15 Jan. 1969, p. 878; Lady Bird Johnson, *Texas: A Roadside View* (San Antonio, TX: Trinity University Press, 1981), pp. xix, xx.

33. Johnson, *Texas,* pp. xix–xx.

34. Ibid., p. xxiii.

35. LBJ to Udall, 18 Apr. 1972, Udall Papers; Barbara Klaw, comp., "Lady Bird Johnson Remembers," *American Heritage,* Dec. 1980, p. 6; LBJ to Helen Keel, 7 June 1974, author's collection.

36. Robert L. Hardesty, "With Lyndon Johnson in Texas: A Memoir of the Post-Presidential Years," in *Farewell to the Chief: Former Presidents in American Public Life,* ed. Richard Norton Smith and Timothy Walch (Worland, WY: High Plains Publishing, 1990), p. 99 (second quotation), and p. 101 (first quotation).

37. Jan Jarboe, "Lady Bird Looks Back," p. 148.

38. Ibid.

39. Harry Middleton, *Lady Bird Johnson: A Life Well Lived* (Austin, TX: The Lyndon Baines Johnson Foundation, 1992), p. 149.

40. Mrs. Lyndon B. Johnson, Remarks at the LBJ Library, 20 Oct. 1988, pp. 8–9, courtesy of Harry Middleton.

41. Lee Kelly, "Lady Bird Renews Commitment at 70," *Austin* (TX) *American-Statesman,* 22 Dec. 1982; and Cheryl Coggins, "70th Birthday Blooms in Joy for Lady Bird," ibid., 23 Dec. 1982.

42. "Lady Bird," *Austin American Statesman,* 20 Dec. 1987.

43. "Wildflower Research Center Seeks Funds to Build New Site," *Austin Weekly,* 12 June 1991.

44. Janet Wilson, "Lady Bird Seizes the Day," *Austin American-Statesman,* 21 Dec. 1997.

45. Middleton, *Lady Bird Johnson,* p. 174.

46. *Wildflower: Lady Bird Johnson Wildflower Center,* May/June 1998, p. 5.

47. Catriona Glazebrook and Bob L. Warneke, "Devotion to Beauty," *Austin American-Statesman,* 9 Jan. 1999; Ralph K. M. Jaurwitz, "Mrs. Johnson's Conservation Work Honored," *Austin American-Statesman,* 15 Jan. 1999.

48. Wilson, "Lady Bird Seizes the Day."

BIBLIOGRAPHIC ESSAY

MANUSCRIPTS

Lady Bird Johnson's personal papers and the manuscript diary of her White House years are not yet open for research, but there is an ample amount of documentary information about her in the papers and files of the Lyndon Baines Johnson Presidential Library in Austin, Texas. For a convenient brief summary of the material the LBJ Library and other libraries have about Mrs. Johnson, researchers should consult the web page of the "First Ladies Library" in Canton, Ohio, at www.firstladies.org.

For Lady Bird Johnson's years as First Lady, the main files to examine are the White House Social Files (WHSF) and the relevant series within that very large category. For her beautification work, the Beautification Files (BF) contain seventeen boxes of important documents about the First Lady's Committee for a More Beautiful Capital, her projects in Washington, and her role in national environmental issues.

Equally useful within the Social Files are Liz Carpenter's Alphabetical Files (LCAF), 129 boxes, and her Subject Files (LCSF), 88 boxes. The Subject Files are illuminating about the trips that Mrs. Johnson took as First Lady. The Alphabetical Files comprise 2,142 boxes, a significant number of which are now open to scholars. This latter file contains much of Mrs. Johnson's personal correspondence during her time as First Lady.

Within the Lyndon Johnson Papers, her letters are represented throughout the Lyndon B. Johnson Archives (LBJA), most especially in 1942 and 1955. The House of Representatives Papers (JHP), 1937–1949, contain an even larger number of her letters for this period. The papers for the vice-president and the postpresidential years are only partially opened. For the presidency, researchers should look at the President's File, PP5/Lady Bird Johnson, and such specific subjects as Arts (AR), Highways–Bridges (HI), Legislation (LE), Parks–Monuments (PA), Public Relations (PR), and Transportation (TN).

The papers of White House aides offer much good material on the First Lady. The most important of these are Douglass Cater, Richard N. Goodwin, Mike Manatos, Harry McPherson, and Bill Moyers. Also helpful are Horace

Busby, Joseph Califano, James Gaither, Robert L. Hardesty, Charles A. Horsky, John W. Macy Jr., Matthew Nimetz, Lawrence F. O'Brien, DeVier Pierson, Irvine Sprague, and Henry Wilson Jr.

Personal papers of use at the library are those of Alan S. Boyd, Nash Castro, and Barefoot Sanders. The Lewis L. Gould Papers contain copies of legal records for Mrs. Johnson's family from Harrison County, along with records on the Johnsons from Blanco and Gillespie Counties in the Hill Country.

Oral histories at the Johnson Library are another important source of insights and information about Lady Bird Johnson and her service as First Lady. The most significant are those of Bess Abell, Liz Carpenter, Nash Castro, Elizabeth Rowe, Phillip Tocker, Stewart Udall, and Cynthia Wilson.

Private papers outside the Johnson Library that are relevant to Mrs. Johnson's tenure as First Lady include Katherine Louchheim and Nathaniel Owings, Library of Congress; Maurine Neuberger, University of Oregon; Lee Metcalf, Montana Historical Society; John Sherman Cooper, University of Kentucky; Stewart Udall, University of Arizona; and Ruth Montgomery, Baylor University. Lawrence Halprin and Cynthia Wilson kindly shared materials from their private files with me.

BIOGRAPHIES AND SECONDARY WORKS

Lady Bird Johnson has written, coauthored, or contributed to several works that shed light on her years as First Lady and her environmental interests. The most important of these is *A White House Diary* (New York: Holt, Rinehart and Winston, 1970), which is a unique document in the literature on First Ladies. For her relations with her husband's presidency it is continually valuable; the coverage of beautification is more spotty. The full diary will become available some years after Mrs. Johnson's death. Lady Bird Johnson has written *Texas: A Roadside View* (San Antonio, TX: Trinity University Press, 1981) and, with Carlton Lees, *Wildflowers Across America* (New York: Abbeville Press, 1988).

Although Lady Bird Johnson has not written an autobiographical volume, there are interviews and articles that provide her own interpretation of her life and work. See Lady Bird Johnson, "When I Was Sixteen," *Good Housekeeping,* October 1968, p. 98; the interview with Mrs. Johnson in Katie Louchheim, ed., *The New Deal: The Insiders Speak* (Cambridge: Harvard University Press, 1983); Barbara Klaw, comp., "Lady Bird Johnson Remembers," *American Heritage,* December 1980, pp. 4–17; Nancy Kegan Smith, "On Being First Lady: An Interview with Lady Bird Johnson," *Prologue* 19 (summer 1987): 136–41; and Jan Jarboe, "Lady Bird Looks Back," *Texas Monthly,* December 1994, pp. 114–17,

142–48. *Addresses by the First Lady, Mrs. Lyndon Baines Johnson, 1964* is a small pamphlet of her speeches available from the LBJ Library.

There is no full biography based on Mrs. Johnson's personal papers. Some popular books appeared during the 1960s, including Ruth Montgomery, *Mrs. LBJ* (New York: Holt, Rinehart and Winston, 1964); Marie Smith, *The President's Lady: An Intimate Biography of Mrs. Lyndon B. Johnson* (New York: Random House, 1964); Frances S. Leighton and Helen Baldwin, *They Call Her Lady Bird* (New York: McFadden-Bartell, 1964); and Gordon Langley Hall, *Lady Bird and Her Daughters* (Philadelphia: Macrae Smith, 1967). Charman Simon's, *Lady Bird Johnson: Making Our Neighborhoods Beautiful* (New York: Children's Press, 1998) is a biography for young people. Harry Middleton's, *Lady Bird Johnson: A Life Well Lived* (Austin, TX: Lyndon Baines Johnson Foundation, 1992) is a pictorial biography with reminiscences by her friends and colleagues. There are two film biographies, one done by the Thaxton Green Studios for the National Park Service and the other for the Arts and Entertainment Biography series, both of which came out in 1998.

A large number of articles about Lady Bird Johnson appeared in the 1960s. Among the most useful are Flora Reta Schreiber, "Lady Bird Johnson's First Years of Marriage," *Woman's Day*, December 1967, pp. 38–39, 91; Blake Clark, "Lyndon Johnson's Lady Bird," *Reader's Digest*, November 1963, pp. 108–13; Nan Robertson, "Our New First Lady," *Saturday Evening Post*, 8 February 1964, pp. 20–25; Katie Louchheim, "Her Interest Is People," *Ladies Home Journal*, March 1964, pp. 56, 126; "I Don't Consider Myself Dull at All: The Real Lady Bird Johnson," *National Observer*, 24 April 1967; Shana Alexander, "Best First Lady," *Life*, 13 December 1968, p. 22b.

Lady Bird Johnson's life is examined in the context of her husband's career in the many biographies of Lyndon B. Johnson that have appeared. These include Robert Caro, *The Years of Lyndon Johnson: The Path to Power* (New York: Alfred A. Knopf, 1982), and *The Years of Lyndon Johnson: Means of Ascent* (New York: Alfred A. Knopf, 1990); Robert Dallek, *Lone Star Rising: Lyndon Johnson and His Times, 1908–1960* (New York: Oxford University Press, 1991), and *Flawed Giant: Lyndon Johnson and His Times, 1961–1973* (New York: Oxford University Press, 1998); and Ronnie Dugger, *The Politician: The Life and Times of Lyndon Johnson* (New York: W. W. Norton, 1982). Mrs. Johnson is also discussed in Vaughn Davis Bornet, *The Presidency of Lyndon B. Johnson* (Lawrence: University Press of Kansas, 1982).

Memoirs of those who knew Lady Bird Johnson are important sources for measuring her influence and understanding her impact on people. Bobby

Baker, *Wheeling and Dealing: Confessions of a Capitol Hill Operator* (New York: W. W. Norton, 1978), offers the recollections of a man close to Lyndon Johnson during the Senate years but should be used with care; Joseph A. Califano, *The Triumph and Tragedy of Lyndon Johnson* (New York: Simon and Schuster, 1991) examines Mrs. Johnson's role in the context of President Johnson's White House performance. Liz Carpenter's, *Ruffles and Flourishes* (College Station: Texas A&M University Press, 1993) is a reprinting of the version that originally appeared in 1969 and 1970. The book contains an abundance of Liz Carpenter's ebullient good humor, but it also sheds a great deal of light on how Mrs. Johnson functioned as First Lady. Katie Louchheim, *By the Political Sea* (Garden City, NY: Doubleday, 1973), provides an account of a longtime Democratic party activist and Washington insider. Nathaniel Alexander Owings, *The Spaces in Between: An Architect's Journey* (Boston: Houghton Mifflin, 1973), describes his work with Mrs. Johnson on Pennsylvania Avenue and other aspects of Washington. James B. West, with Mary Lynn Kotz, *Upstairs at the White House: My Life with the First Ladies* (New York: Coward, McCann and Geoghegan, 1973), offers the insights of the White House usher. Jake Pickle & Peggy Pickle, *Jake* (Austin: University of Texas Press, 1997), offer the recollections of a longtime friend and political ally.

The reporters who covered Lady Bird Johnson commented about her in their own memoirs. Among the most useful are Nancy Dickerson, *Among Those Present: A Reporter's View of Twenty-Five Years in Washington* (New York: Random House, 1976); Maxine Cheshire, with John Greenya, *Maxine Cheshire, Reporter* (Boston: Houghton Mifflin, 1978); Ruth Montgomery, *Hail to the Chiefs* (New York: McCann, 1970); and Helen Thomas, *Dateline White House* (New York: Macmillan, 1975).

The emerging scholarship on First Ladies has devoted attention to Lady Bird Johnson and her role and includes Carl Sferrazza Anthony, *First Ladies: The Saga of the Presidents' Wives and Their Power* (New York: William Morrow, 1990); Betty Caroli, *First Ladies* (New York: Oxford University Press, 1986); Myra Gutin, *The President's Partner: The First Lady in the Twentieth Century* (Westport, CT: Greenwood Press, 1989); and Gil Troy, *Affairs of State: The Rise and Rejection of the Presidential Couple Since World War II* (New York: Free Press, 1997). I contributed an essay about Mrs. Johnson to *American First Ladies: Their Lives and Their Legacy,* ed. Lewis L. Gould (New York: Garland Publishing, 1996).

On the specific issues that Lady Bird Johnson dealt with as First Lady, the amount of relevant scholarly writing is not large. June Sochen, *Movers and*

Shakers: American Women Thinkers and Activists, 1900–1970 (New York: Quadrangle, 1973), has an early and perceptive appraisal of Mrs. Johnson's work. For the environmental campaigns in the Johnson White House, see Martin V. Melosi, "Lyndon Johnson and Environmental Policy," in *The Johnson Years,* ed. Robert A. Divine, vol. 2 (Lawrence: University Press of Kansas, 1987), pp. 113–49; Samuel P. Hays, *Beauty, Health, and Permanence* (New York: Cambridge University Press, 1987); Hal Rothman, *The Greening of a Nation? Environmentalism in the United States Since 1945* (Fort Worth, TX: Harcourt Brace, 1998); Susan R. Schrepfer, *The Fight to Save the Redwoods: A History of Environmental Reform, 1917–1978* (Madison: University of Wisconsin Press, 1983); Robin Winks, *Laurance S. Rockefeller: Catalyst for Conservation* (Washington, DC: Island Press, 1997). Useful on related aspects of Mrs. Johnson's work in the White House are Susan M. Hartmann, "Women's Issues and the Johnson Administration," in Divine, ed., *The Johnson Years,* vol. 3, *LBJ at Home and Abroad* (Lawrence: University Press of Kansas, 1994), 53–81, Irving Bernstein, *Guns or Butter: The Presidency of Lyndon Johnson* (New York: Oxford University Press, 1996), and John A. Andrew III, *Lyndon Johnson and the Great Society* (Chicago: Ivan Dee, 1998).

The history of billboard control has not yet been written. John W. Houck, *Outdoor Advertising: History and Regulation* (Notre Dame, IN: Notre Dame University Press, 1969), offers an essential starting point. Charles F. Floyd and Peter J. Shedd, *Highway Beautification: The Environmental Movement's Greatest Failure* (Boulder, CO: Westview Press, 1979), provide the antibillboard critique of the 1965 legislation. William H. Wilson, "The Billboard: Bane of the City Beautiful," *Journal of Urban History* 13 (August 1987): 394–425, looks at the origins of the billboard-control campaign. Cynthia Meyers, "Godfrey Flury's Billboard Advertising Business: An Austin Ad Man in the 1910s and 1920s," *Southwestern Historical Quarterly* 98 (April 1995): 569–83, provides background on the rise of the outdoor advertising industry in Mrs. Johnson's home state. Don Phillip, "A Bumpy Ride for Highway Cleanup: Environmental Group Says Billboards Have Proliferated Under 1965 Law," *Washington Post,* 25 April 1997, gives the most recent unfavorable assessment of the measure. The antibillboard group Scenic America monitors the Highway Beautification Act and its enforcement at www.landscapeonline.com.

For Washington, DC and its history, recent studies are Howard Gillette, *Between Justice and Beauty: Race, Planning, and the Failure of Urban Policy in Washington, D.C.* (Baltimore: Johns Hopkins University Press, 1995), and Harry Jaffe, *Dream City: Race, Power, and the Decline of Washington, D.C.* (New York:

Simon and Schuster, 1994). Former mayor Walter Washington is reported to be writing his memoirs about his years in District politics. Barry Hyams's, *Hirsh-horn: Medici from Brooklyn* (New York: Dutton, 1979) is useful for Mrs. Johnson's role in the creation of the museum that bears its donor's name.

An impressive number of student papers, theses, and dissertations bear on Lady Bird Johnson's career. Unless otherwise indicated, they can be found in the University of Texas Library through the computerized catalog at www.utexas. edu.: Deborah Bannworth, "Lady Bird Johnson's Tenure in the Congressional Office," course paper, 1986, University of Texas at Austin, LBJL; Laura Susan Beilharz, "The Unique Influence and Tremendous Impact of Mrs. Lyndon Baines Johnson on Operation Head Start," seminar paper, 1986; Elvia Garcia, "Lady Bird Johnson: Whistle Stopping Through the South," senior thesis, 1986; Norma Ruth Holly Foreman, "The First Lady as a Leader of Public Opinion: A Study of the Role and Press Relations of Lady Bird Johnson" (Ph.D diss., University of Texas at Austin, 1971); Angela Landon, "We Meet in Grief: The Relationship Between Jacqueline Kennedy and Lyndon Johnson," course paper, 1992; Lara Elizabeth Pechard, "First Ladies and *Life*—The Politics of Gender Representation in the American Popular Press" (master's thesis, University of Southhampton, 1998), copy courtesy of the author, who uses Mrs. Johnson as one of her case studies; Beverly Smith Wakefield, "The Speechmaking of Mrs. Lyndon Baines Johnson, January 1964–April 1968" (Master's thesis, University of Texas at Austin, 1968). Janet Mezzack's, " 'Without manners you are nothing': Lady Bird Johnson, Eartha Kitt, and the Women Doers Luncheon of January 18, 1968," *Presidential Studies Quarterly* 20 (fall 1990): 745–61 is a revised version of another student essay.

INDEX